THE LAST

THE LAST WELSH SUMMER

Catherine Johnson

Pont Books

First Publication—1993
This edition—May 1996

ISBN 1 85902 017 8

© Catherine Johnson

All rights reserved. No part of this book may be reproduced, stored in a retrieval system, or transmitted in any form or by any means, electronic, electrostatic, magnetic tape, mechanical, photocopying, recording or otherwise, without permission in writing from the publishers, Gomer Press, Llandysul, Dyfed

Printed in Wales at
Gomer Press, Llandysul, Dyfed

1

The three of them had got out of the Tube at Notting Hill—Hector in front, tall and gangling, resplendent in his newest tracksuit, a little ahead of his sister, Cecile, and her schoolfriend, Suki. Although he had agreed to bring them and 'keep an eye on them', he was already regretting walking up the Portobello Road with his little sister, and having to turn round and yell 'Come on!' at them every few yards as they looked at stalls and in clothes shop windows. He had told them that when they got to the record shop they weren't to show him up in front of his mates, but he could see he was heading for trouble.

It was a crush moving through the busy street market. The girls could just about make out Hector's dark baseball cap bobbing easily through the crowd. But there was so much to look at, more than Southall market, and it was ten times more alive than the sanitized Ealing shopping centre, where the girls would hang about after school sometimes. The market was a mixture of antiques, through to junk, through to bag ladies selling their last belongings spread out on a tea towel for twenty pence. There were also fruit and veg stalls, hippy shops, rasta shops, clothes shops, everything.

Suki could see every sort of person: tourists dripping with cameras, rastas, trendies, all shades of weirdo, kids and adults rummaging in the roadside for fallen fruit and vegetables. Music, noise, colour.

Everything was louder and brighter. And in the sun, the smell of crushed, decomposing fruit and the stickiness of the pavements half reminded her of the family trip to Guyana three years ago.

'Suks! Come on!' Now it was Cecile, tugging at her T-shirt; Hector had disappeared down a turning up ahead. Their pace changed, and the two girls wove quickly through the crowd with the ease of City girls. Elbows, after all, were for elbowing. And they quickly remembered that only tourists, (and homegirls up from the suburbs) were uncool enough to dawdle.

It was easy enough to spot the record shop from the giant speaker sat on the pavement, thudding out music and on the door a poster for a pre-Carnival dance. Inside, Hector, visible through the glass, was meeting friends, talking right up to each other's ears so as to hear above the noise. Cecile marched straight in, cross with Hector for not waiting.

'Hang on!' Suki called to her, 'I'm just going in this shop next door. I'll catch you in a minute.'

Next door to the record shop was a book shop. It had the same Carnival poster on its door as the record shop. Painted onto the glass window in bright yellow and black were the words, 'New Horizons Afro-Caribbean Bookshop'. The words made it hard to see inside, and Suki craned her neck to see in round the letters before pushing the door open and going inside.

Half an hour later, it was Cecile and Hector who had to come looking for her, dragging her away from the shelves of books and making her choose which ones she was actually going to buy. She came away with *Black Heroes in the Hall of Fame, from Pushkin and Mary Seacole to Marcus Garvey* and *A History of Slavery in the West Indies*. She couldn't afford any records after that.

On the Tube on the way back Hector was winding her up rotten. 'What's up with her, Cile? Is she going home to raise her black consciousness?' He was giggling and smiling and singing 'Zippin' up my boots, Goin' back to my roots, Yeah!'

'Oh shut up, Hector!' Cecile was still cross with him for not letting them stay longer.

But Suki didn't care. Apart from being used to Hector's teasing, she was too pleased with her books, and was only annoyed because she couldn't think of something suitably withering to say in return.

But now Hector had snatched her bag and was reading her book titles in a silly voice, out loud on the Tube train.

'Give them back Hector, don't be stupid!' She was aware that her voice had suddenly leapt an octave and become that of a squeaky girl.

Hector jumped into the seat next to her, and grinning, whispered in her ear, 'Didn't you ever look in the mirror when you were a lickle ickle girl, and realise it was not going to wash off?'

For a minute Suki was dumbstruck, then before she knew what had happened Cecile in one deft movement had sat on his lap and pulled the fingers of his right hand down and round into a finger lock, a technique Suki had seen her use before on her brother when they got into fights. She marched him over to his own seat and threatened to sit on his new records unless he behaved.

They were all giggling by now—Hector, in between his cries of 'Ow, ow you really hurt me', feigning fear of his younger sister, and Suki watching them, wishing she was not an only child.

When they parted a little way from the station, Suki began to think about what Hector had said. He didn't know how close he was to the truth. Of course Suki had known that her skin wasn't white, but she had never thought of herself as Black. Her skin colour, that of strongish tea with milk, and her hair, coarse black, not quite afro, were a minor genetic blip, though not one she denied. It was just not what made her special. What made her different, unique, was that she had believed she was Welsh. All along from as far back as she could remember she had been Welsh. Until last year, that is.

Suki turned the corner into her road, a tidy redbrick terraced street with tall plane trees and neat little identical houses. Theirs was the one with the bottle green door and the plants in the front window; her mum was good with plants. Even before she had opened the door she could hear her mum talking on the phone to Auntie Ceinwen in Welsh, shrieking and hooting and making preparations for their three week holiday in France together. Without children and without men.

Suki had made up her mind. She gripped the bag

from the bookshop and mouthed silently to her mother, 'I'm not going to Nain's!' But her mum hadn't noticed at all; she was deep in conversation. Suki turned and ran up the stairs, slamming her bedroom door.

As it was Saturday, one of Dad's cooking days, they were having one of his specials, steaming hot curried chicken. Some of Mum's friends from work were coming too, and Suki was in the kitchen helping him.

'Dad?' It was that long inquisitive 'Da-ad' that meant Suki was after something. 'Dad, you know when Mum goes to France next week?' Suki paused, hoping she'd get the words out right.

'Yes?' Joshua was chopping up some garlic and listening intently to the cricket on the radio at the same time.

'Well,' Suki continued, 'couldn't I stay here with you instead of going to Nain's?'

Her Dad waited to hear DeFreitas caught before answering. 'Look, love, you know I'll be on nights half the time your mother's away. We can't leave you on your own at night, can we?'

He was talking to her like she was nine. Suki reacted like a nine year old, sighing loudly and avoiding his gaze by staring out into the garden.

'Anyway, what's up with your Nain's all of a sudden, eh? You love it up there!'

Suki's voice went into top gear, into whine mode, 'Oh Dad! It's different now, isn't it?'

The crowd on the radio roared for a six and

Joshua smiled, scraping the garlic off the chopping board and into the pan. 'What? What's different?' He was only half listening: the cricket match was getting interesting.

'It's just not the same. My friends are all down here Dad, and anyway, I wanted to go to Carnival with Cecile this year. Couldn't I stay at her house? I'm sure her mum wouldn't mind. Would you ask Mum for me, please? Would you, Dad?'

Unfortunately for Suki, her mother had caught the end of the conversation and was clicking across the quarry tiled floor with an armful of flowers to put into vases. 'Ask me what, love? Hmm?'

'Nothing, Mum.' Suddenly grinding up allspice seemed totally absorbing.

It had always been harder to get her own way with her mother. Going through her Dad seemed easier —getting him to do the difficult bit.

Joshua dissected the yellow corn-fed chicken, twisting the leg and cutting it free of the hip socket. He paused, looking across to his wife. 'Something about Wales—the holiday, wasn't it, Suks?'

'It'll wait, Dad', she replied, in her best, 'it doesn't matter' voice.

'But love, it's next week. It can't wait too much longer.' Her mother was concerned; she didn't want anything ruining her break with Ceinwen.

'I doubt if the Juliennes would have you at such short notice anyway.' He began sawing through the chicken's breast bone now, with a shiny French kitchen knife, opening the bird up flat. Suki's stomach turned. It looked like a survivor of some massacre somewhere. Poor jaundiced dead thing. She was glad she had become a vegetarian. Now she could not tear her eyes away from the sorry looking yellow chicken as her Dad pulled and scraped the breast meat away from the bone.

'I don't want to go, Mum. I want to stay in London this year and go to the Carnival with Cecile.' She was still staring at the chicken. 'We'd be OK. Hector and Valentine, Cile's brothers, they'd look after us!'

Her mother was confused, not really listening.

'What? Which Carnival? Here this summer? I thought the council had cut the Carnival a couple of years ago!'

Suki smiled broadly at her mother's ignorance. 'No, Mum, not in Ealing. Honestly, Mother! The big one—Notting Hill, of course!'

Her mother didn't even pause long enough to consider it. 'You don't really think . . . two thirteen year old girls. No Suki, there's no way we'd let you go.'

'But mother, we're both nearly fourteen, and like I said her brothers . . .'

'No, Suki. Anyway it's not just that, though God knows I'd be unhappy about you going to that Carnival. What about Nain and Taid? You love it up there, don't you?'

'Mother!' They were not even taking it seriously. She stormed out of the kitchen and up to her bedroom.

Deep down she knew it wouldn't work and she'd have to go up to Wales but she wanted so much to stay in London. For the *first time* she wanted to stay in London. As she lay on her bed she could hear her parents' voices wafting up from the kitchen through her open window.

'Josh, I'm not having her going to Notting Hill Carnival on her own, not at thirteen. There's riots and everything!'

Even though Suki was on the verge of tears it made her smile to hear her smart *Guardian*-reading radio 4-producer mother reduced to spouting tabloid newspaperspeak.

'Riots!' Suki found herself answering, shouting out loud. 'There haven't been any riots for years and YEARS!'

They just didn't understand that things had changed. '*I've* changed!' She was talking out loud, safe in the knowledge that they couldn't hear her. Every year she felt more and more different from Nia, her cousin, from Nain and Taid and Heulwen Haf, her aunt. It used to be that she felt a part of everything up there. Now she felt like she was watching television. Sometimes, worst of all, she felt just like another 'visitor'.

In London with Cecile, she felt like she belonged. London didn't use to feel like home, especially once she started secondary school. Suki went to this anachronism of a girls' grammer school, one of the handful remaining in London. The register was stuffed with Charlottes and Georginas, every derivative of Kate and Sarah. True, there were quite a few Sitas and Fozias, but she and Cecile were the only black girls in her year.

Cecile's family seemed exciting and vigorous, compared with the calm of her well ordered, always tidy, cleaning-lady-cleaned home. Why couldn't she stay with them this summer? It wasn't fair. She could hear her mother's answer before she asked: 'Life isn't fair, love.'

2

It was at the very end of the holiday last year that the change in her had started. It was evening, still light, but wouldn't be for long. They were all sitting on the village playing-field, talking. The playing-field was just that, a scrubby field sloping up the hill at the back of the village, with an old witch's hat, some rusty swings, and, fair dos, a brand new slide and climbing frame nestling on a bed of dark brown bark chips.

Iola Mary and Wendy were sitting on the two best swings, the metal chains creaking, pretending to inhale Benson and Hedges King Size. Sarah Howell from the village shop and Nia sat on the other two swings, while the younger and less favoured girls, Meinir, Suki and Iola's little sister Eirlys, were relegated to the witch's hat. Eirlys, who was nine, was only hanging around with the older girls because she had threatened to tell on Iola Mary for smoking, and to tell the truth she found them more than a little boring. All they ever did was sit around and chat. Though sometimes Meinir and Suki would help her make dens.

The telephone wires were heavy with swallows, wondering whether they should leave now or chance the British summer for another week. Suki and Nia didn't have the choice: they were going back to Llandudno in the morning, and Suki would be back in London by the end of the week.

'I wish we could stay!' Suki was leaning off the seat of the witch's hat picking up stones, then letting them fall through her fingers.

'You always say that. Every year. I'd much rather live in London, all those shops!' Iola Mary's idea of London was one huge Miss Selfridge next door to an equally huge McDonalds.

Nia wasn't listening. 'I can't wait!' she sighed, looking across to the village.

'Aaah, poor Ni,' Sarah was teasing. 'How do all your poor little pony friends manage without you!'

Sarah and Iola started singing 'My Little Pony.' Nia sat up smiling, even though it was an old joke, and threw some plantain heads at them.

Wendy wasn't listening either. 'I think I'll get my hair cut before school, just about here. What d'you think, Io?' she was holding her long brown hair between her fingers, at about chin level.

'School! Aagh! Do you have to remind me?' Iola Mary leant over the side of the swing and pretended to be sick. Wendy and Sarah giggled.

'But there's always Mr Huws,' reminded Wendy.

'Who's he?' asked Nia.

'Oh,' answered Sarah, 'he's the new Welsh teacher, started last Christmas. Every girl in the third year is totally mad on him!'

Nia was unimpressed. 'Poor bloke, with you lot, all cow-eyed over him!'

'Just 'cause he's not a horse, Nia Roberts. Honestly! When will you grow up?' Nia ignored that last remark. Iola Mary could be quite spiteful when she felt like it.

'Anyway, he's practically married!' sighed Wendy, blowing smoke high into the air.

'Hey Suki, we saw his girlfriend at the end-of-term fair, she's—you know—black!' Sarah was enthusiastic.

'So? What's that to me?' Suki was uneasy.

'My mum says she only got that job 'cause she's black!' Wendy was smug.

'What job? Mr Huws's girlfriend?'

Even Suki laughed.

'No, Io, you idiot! That job with S4C in Caernarfon! My mum knows all about it!'

'Well she would, wouldn't she, Wend!' Iola Mary never liked anyone knowing more about anything than herself.

Sarah was adamant: 'Well anyway, she *is* Welsh. She's from Swansea or something. I spoke to her, and she was very nice.'

A look of total disbelief came over Wendy's face, 'Don't be stupid, Sarah. How can she be Welsh?' She took another puff and turned to Iola Mary for backup. 'She can't be, can she, Io?'

Suki felt hotness in her cheeks, and her eyes began to smart. Why did she have to be different?

Iola looked thoughtful, 'I s'pose not. I don't know.'

'Oh Iola, how can she be black and Welsh? She's foreign, isn't she? Honestly!' Wendy threw the cigarette butt down and ground it under her foot decisively.

Nia suddenly felt defensive, 'Hey! Come on, Wend, what about Suki?'

'What about her?' Wendy stared at Suki. She was spoiling for a fight. Suki looked up from the ground and stared right back. Wendy gave Iola Mary a dig in the ribs—they could have a laugh now. Suki was so easy to wind up.

'Look, this is stupid! What does it matter anyway?' Sarah didn't want this. She wasn't into being spiteful for a bit of fun. She tried changing the subject. 'Dad said some new people are going to buy Ty'n Llidiart.'

It didn't work.

'Suki's all right.' It was Iola, smirking. 'I mean, you're not black, not Black black, more sort of, um, mid brown, if you know what I mean.'

Iola Mary and Wendy looked at each other, trying not to giggle, then Wendy spoke,

'I mean, you're not white either, are you? You're not like us.'

'Stop it, Wendy!' hissed Nia.

Suki was not saying anything. She was racking her brain trying to think of something, anything, but it was hard enough just to stop the tears starting.

Suki got up and started walking for the gate, walking faster and faster until she was almost running. Nia got up to go after her. 'Look what you've done now, Wendy. I hope you're pleased with yourself!'

Wendy shouted after them, 'It's only a laugh! Your cousin doesn't have to be so bloody touchy!'

Suki expected that everyone else had forgotten that day, but that was it. That was when she realised what she had half known, but had now had spelt out for her— that she was not Welsh.

Every holiday longer than a week, and some half terms too when Mum was busy, she had been packed off to Auntie Ceinwen's, and then to Nain and Taid's with her cousins. Suki had always imagined herself living up there one day. Now she could kick herself for being so stupid. She would never fit in. 'Coffee' didn't sound like such a cute nickname anymore. She was a Londoner, a Black girl, whatever anyone said, whatever 'hybrid vigour' her Mum said she had. And she didn't even have to open her mouth.

3

Nia Roberts slid to a halt, the gravel on the little path working its way into her sandals and in between her toes. She leant the bike, an old one of her sister's, up against the kitchen door and flopped into the kitchen, pausing only to deposit an old plastic bag containing her much encrusted jodphur boots, just inside the downstairs toilet door.

She was bright red in the face, partly from the three mile bike ride, partly from spending every available Saturday, Sunday and summer evening up at the stables. The skin on her nose was just starting to peel, showing pinky freckledness underneath. She kicked off her ropey old flip flops, sending them skidding over the lino, then padded over to the fridge for a carton of fruit juice. She drank, her eyes almost glazed over—she was so tired. She was filthy, sweaty and smelly, and her hair, which when washed was a pleasing light chestnutty brown, was stuck to her head in some places and in others had assumed the shape of her riding hat.

'Ni!' She heard her Mum coming down the stairs. 'Is that you, love? Give us a hand with this bloody hat.' Her mother, already looking slightly harassed, as if harassment were a natural accessory to the navy blue polyester uniform she wore, entered the kitchen. She was attempting to pin one of those ridiculous rudimentary nurses' hats made of plasticised cardboard onto her head. She looked at Nia, whose hands were brown with dirt. 'Oh, and wash your hands first, Ni.'

Nia sat her Mum down, and quickly and deftly pinned on the offending hat, as she did at least three times a week before her mum went off to work in the 'Awel-y-Môr' nursing home in Deganwy. She did Sundays sometimes too. It made her tired and she moaned about it, usually in the morning as Ni and Rhys were getting ready for school. She drew on the last cigarette of her day, advocating wholesale euthanasia and complaining about the geriatrics. Rhys laughed callously along with her. Then seeing Nia's face, her mother would add, 'Oh, love! I don't mean it!' Nia hated it when her Mum talked about work like this—it made her feel responsible. Responsible and guilty. If she was older she could get a job. It had been easier and simpler before Dad left.

Nia examined her mother's face and bit her tongue. She was going to ask about staying at home, and getting her best friend Ceri Wynne to come and stay while Mum was in France, and yes she knew Nain was expecting her. And that Mum didn't want two fourteen year olds running riot in her house for three weeks. And that it was different for Rhys 'because he's older'. But just before work was never the right time. Instead Nia smiled a feeble goodbye smile at her Mum and watched as she pulled on her jacket and shouted for Rhys to come and give her a lift.

Rhys thundered down the stairs like a lead-booted diver. Ceinwen winced as she imagined the wear on the already-past-it stair carpet. Rhys was not a pretty sight; large and seemingly unco-ordinated, scruffy in his metal-thrash-biker uniform of ancient torn denim and mock gothic T-shirt. Nia, slumped over the juice carton, made a face at her brother, angry with him for being seventeen and allowed to do as he wanted.

'What's up with the troll?' Rhys patted Nia on the head. 'Fell off your horse?' Nia threw a flip-flop at him as he escaped through the door, jangling his car keys.

Nia heard his Hillman Minx judder, once, twice, then burst into life and put-put off down the road. She took up the juice carton and went up the stairs to her bedroom. Old Hwmby, the cat her sister Lowri saved from an untimely end in Taid's bucket one summer, was curled up, dribbly and crosslooking in the middle of her bed. Nia had never liked him. His breath smelt and he bit. 'Move off, you stupid cat.' She took her filthy jodphurs off and flung them at him. Hwmby scurried off under Lo's bed on the other side of the room, hissing.

With Lo away at university the bedroom seemed bigger, but Nia missed her. 'If she was here this summer, instead of travelling somewhere, Mum'd let me stay. I know it.'

In the dressing-table drawer there was a set of those photo-booth photos Lowri took of herself in Llandudno Woolworths. Ni took them out and looked first at them, and then at herself in the mirror. Lo was tall, not quite willowy, but stately and very good looking, like Mum when she was young. Nia was tall too, but still quite heavy with puppy fat. Big-boned, her mother called her, trying to be kind.

There was a picture of Dad in Nia's drawer too, but not in Lowri's. She said she hated him for leaving Mum and that she wouldn't have anything to do with him. She always tore up birthday cards and letters, even if they'd got money in them. She and Ni had had a big row one year when Nia had written to him asking for a new riding hat.

'How could you, Ni, after what he did to Mum, to us?'

Lo had found the unfinished letter, and was waving it in front of her face shouting.

Nia was red-faced, half sobbing. 'It's different for me, Lo! I liked him.'

'Liked him! God, Nia, you really don't understand. He left Mum, us, he couldn't care less!'

Just thinking about it made her feel uneasy. She hadn't seen her Dad for three years now, and he only lived forty or so miles away in Corwen. Birthday and Christmas cards and parcels would arrive, always the same, a five pound note and a furry toy. About two years ago the furry toy had become bubble bath and talc sets. That was when she'd written asking for the riding hat, and Lo was right. It was stupid. What had he ever done for her? But Nia had only been six when he left. She could only remember all five of them on the beach, like in the holiday snaps downstairs, or Dad coming in from work and lifting her up and twirling her round. She never remembered the rows.

Suddenly she heard the door slam. Rhys was home again. She scooped the photos back into the drawer, pulled on a pair of old saggy-kneed leggings and went down to talk to him.

'Rhys!'

Rhys was sitting on the sofa in front of the telly with his feet up, eating sardines out of the tin, spooning the occasional fish out into a saucer on the floor for Hwmby.

'Oh, Rhys! Can't you feed that animal in the kitchen?' Great globs of oil were trickling out of the corner of his mouth, and hanging off the prongs of his fork, waiting to drip onto the carpet. 'You are disgusting, brother. If your darling Beca could see you now she'd chuck you this minute!'

'Dear little sister,' He turned away from the telly to look at her, talking through a mouthful of viscous sardine, 'you do not, as yet, understand the true nature of love.'

'Then I think I'll stick with horses.'

'No one else would have you!'

Nia picked up the chair cushion and hurled it at him.

'Careful!' Rhys and sardine-tin ducked, sending a stream of yellow fishy oil flying across Hwmby and the sofa. 'Now look what you've made me do! Come on, clear it up. Mum'll kill us. The whole place will stink of fish!'

Nia took no notice. 'Ha! That'll teach you not to eat in the sitting room then!'

The phone rang, and as usual it was Ceri. Nia escaped from the fish odour into the hall and sat on the floor, up against the wall in the dark.

'No, Cer, I'll have to go. I really don't see any way out. Mum's really looking forward to this holiday. I can't muck it up for her.'

'Oh, Ni, it's not fair, Rhys can stay and you can't!'

'Don't remind me! And there's only one week of the holidays left when I get back. Three weeks I'll be gone for! Those ponies will have forgotten who I am, and I bet Mrs Pritchard gets another helper in instead of me!' Nia sighed. 'Oh, it's just not worth even thinking about!'

Later in bed, Nia comforted herself with the thought that she only had two more years at school, then she could jack it all in and get a job as working pupil at a riding school or livery yard somewhere. Then it would be horses all year round and no packing her off to Llŷn with her baby cousin. Mrs Pritchard at the stables had often, well once or twice, said she was good enough. And she was not the GCSE and A levels type. It was hard being the youngest and the thickest, especially when Lo and Rhys were so effortlessly clever, and everyone expected her to be the same. She tried to clear her mind for sleep, but that was an effort too.

It was not fair, not at all fair.

4

Suki had walked over to Cecile's to say goodbye that morning, borrowed a couple of tapes to take with her, and was now at home again, helping her mother load up the car.

'Darling, do we have to take your bike? There are plenty of old ones hanging around your Nain's.'

'But, Mum, they always have punctures and weigh about half a ton, and they never have any gears!'

Suki was proud of her bike, new last Christmas, a mountain bike, with copious gears, and bright purple. Her Mother was less than keen to take it. Apart from the bother of strapping it to the roof of the small car, she would feel guilty at Suki flashing her expensive bike in front of her sister's kids. On Ceinwen's wages things were always tight, especially with three kids, and one at university. It was Dilys herself who was paying Ceinwen's share of the holiday and it would be the first time Ceinwen had ever been abroad.

Once the car was piled up and they'd said goodbye to Dad, the little car pulled off, out of leafy Ealing, through what was left of the factories around London and onto the motorway. It was motorway all the way now, even once they got to Wales.

When Suki was younger they used to drive to Auntie Cein's over the moors, and up the Conwy valley, first empty nothingness, then dense, thick, lush green forest and small farms in the flat valley. But now they used the new expressway, all industrial parks and then the coast; forlorn, grey resorts like Pen-sarn and places with silly names like Mochdre, Pig Town. 'Knocks a whole hour off the journey!'

Her Mum, Dilys, was enthusiastic. To Suki it was still a long drive, and journey's end, at Llandudno Junction, always seemed an anti-climax.

The Roberts's house was one of those standard thirties semis: pebble-dash on the bottom half and mock Tudor fake beams on the top half, on a turning with lots of other identical semis. It could be anywhere, Suki thought, staring out of the car window, as the front door flew open and her Auntie Ceinwen came out to meet them, yelling for Rhys to help with the luggage.

Suki watched as the two sisters hugged, linked

arms, and walked together up the little path to the kitchen door, talking and smiling like schoolgirls. Ceinwen, taller, fairer, and more tired looking than her older, darker, smarter sister. Suki opened the boot and took out a couple of bags, as Rhys loped towards her grinning.

'Hiya, how's the little cousin then?'

'Oi, less of the little!' Suki half swung, half threw a holdall at him playfully, 'Catch!'

Rhys stood there smiling, purposely letting the bag fall to his feet. 'See, I'm useless. Should be able to do it on your own anyway, big woman like you.'

'Oh shut up, Rhys!' Suki smiled at him. He was almost the big brother she never had. Well, except for him being, as she saw it, stuck in some seventies, heavy metal time warp. If only he would do something about those clothes! And that mess on the top of his head that passed for hair. Sometimes it made her shudder just to think she had a blood relation with his taste in music.

They left the bags by the hall door, and when Suki found her mother she was already deep in lost months of gossip with her Aunt.

'You wouldn't think phones had been invented, to look at them!' Rhys was dismissive and bounded quickly back up the stairs to his bedroom.

'Have yourself some tea, love.' Auntie Ceinwen smiled, aunt-like, pausing in mid chat. They were talking very fast in Welsh. Suki could pick up more of it than the sisters realised, but it was of little interest. Work, more work, Rhys not doing as much school work as he should, Rhys spending too much time with this new girlfriend, even if she is very nice, and the daughter of someone big in the council, Nia doing hardly any schoolwork at all, and spending all of her time off with the horses. Where was that going to get her? If only they were all like reliable, responsible, hardworking Lo.

More tea was poured, Suki found herself staring out across the neglected back garden, with its overgrown rockery bit at the end and the huge rusting red swing, slap in the middle of the lawn. The talk started to get more interesting: Auntie Cein's new boyfriend. Suki sat up in her chair, having to concentrate hard to understand what they said. Her mother however sensed Suki's interest.

'Why don't you take your bag up to Nia's room, love? I'm sure she's got some books up there or something.'

'Yeah, great.' Suki was not impressed. *Jills' Super New Pony Wins Everything At An Absolutely Smashing Gymkhana*? Thanks, but no thanks.

Suki smiled at the two women. She knew they wanted to get rid of her, but she didn't really mind.

'Don't worry, I'm going. I'll go and watch the telly in the front room.'

Her Aunt called out after her, 'Nia will be back from the stables in about half an hour!' and then after the kitchen door had shut, 'Will she be alright? She seems a bit down in the dumps?'

'Ah, she's just mithering after the journey!'

Suki shut the sitting room door so that she couldn't

hear them anymore and settled down on the sofa, flicked the telly on and leafed through a pile of magazines on the floor. They ranged from *The Daily Post,* to *Kerrang* to *Pony,* through to the *papur bro*, which consisted mainly of an update on *Merched y Wawr*—women's meetings—and bazaars, who was going to the eisteddfod, and poems sent in by old men. Suki picked it up and tried to understand as much as she could. 'When the Railway came to Ro-wen'. It was not that bad really. And the pictures of all the kids at their end of term sports days. They all had such 'Welsh' Welsh names these days, thought Suki —Einir, Cadfan, Eurgain, Gwydion; maybe their mothers had swallowed copies of *The Mabinogion* during pregnancy.

Suki remembered when she had wanted a Welsh name. Before she was born her mother had wanted her to be called Angharad.

'We couldn't have called you that,' her Dad had said. 'You'd get called hand grenade at school!'

So she had ended up as Sara Susannah Josephs, named for her two grandmothers, one who had died and she'd never met, in Guyana, on the other side of the world. And that's how she felt, looking at these beaming round faces, with their straight hair and fringes and freckles. There was a half of herself she didn't know.

Not like Einir there in the photo, winning the under 16s something-or-other at Eglwysbach. Einir was Welsh, Einir's family had lived in the same house for generations. Einir fitted in, Einir knew who she was.

The slam of the metal gate jolted her out of her daydream. Nia was wheeling her bike round in front of the bay window to the kitchen door, with Ceri in tow. Suki started to get up to go and meet them. Then she could hear them talking and laughing. Nia was nearly a year older than Suki and Suki always felt it. Especially when Ceri was around. The 'In' school and horse jokes they shared sometimes made her feel such a baby. She decided to wait for them, and turned the telly up louder with the remote control.

'Hiya, Mum, Auntie Dilys.'

'Hello, Mrs Roberts'.

The two girls stood in the doorway knocking the gravel out of their flip-flops.

'Suki's in the front room. I'm sure she'd love to see you two.' Even her mother didn't sound convinced. Nia and Ceri exchanged knowing looks. Although she didn't dislike her cousin, Nia often found Suki's know-it-all, seen-it-all, done-it-all attitude wearing. And to be honest it wasn't just that. She envied the newness of her clothes and the un-fatness of her legs. She envied her only-childness and 'happy-two-parent-home'. That wasn't to say they hadn't had fun sometimes. It was just, well, just that they weren't each other's natural choice of friends. And they were both much too old for 'Run along now, and play nicely'.

They managed to politely avoid each other all afternoon, Nia and Ceri up in the bedroom swopping tales of idiotic pony trekkers wearing unsuitable footwear, Suki glued to the sofa in the front room. Just before dinner Ceri left and Beca, Rhys's girlfriend, arrived. She was almost as tall as Rhys with short brown hair. Rhys gazed at her as if he couldn't believe his luck. Nia called it his sick dog look. Nia saw Suki staring and hissed, 'No, I don't know what she sees in him either!' and the two girls smiled at each other. It was a bit easier after that.

'Hey, Nia,' Suki called her over so the others wouldn't hear, 'I didn't want to go either.' Suki paused, and looked straight into Nia's face so she'd believe her. 'I wanted to stay in London.'

Nia said nothing, but she couldn't quite believe her.

5

The old car, heavy with people, bags and bikes, chugged along the coast motorway. Nia and Suki stared out of opposite windows, Nia to the sea, Suki to the towns inland. Beca sat in the passenger seat lighting cigs for Rhys and herself. Rhys occasionally swore when they got stuck behind a caravan

'Bloody tourists!'

Suki sighed a very loud sigh. Penmaen-mawr was grey and unhappy looking, cut in two by the new road. 'These places, they all look the same don't they? These towns, streets, like where you live. I mean it's not really Welsh, is it?'

Beca in mid draw on her cigarette began half-laughing half-sputtering. 'What is your idea of Welsh, then?'

Suki, not noticing the sarcasm in her voice, continued, 'Well you know, stone or whitewash, not pebble dash, and double fronted, symmetrical, you know four windows, slate roof, you know.'

'Oh yes,' said Rhys, mocking, 'and I suppose you'd have us all wearing pointy hats and waving leeks!'

Beca giggled and Nia smirked. Suki was mortified, and hoped the slippery vinyl car seat would swallow her up.

Rhys didn't have a car stereo, but he'd brought his portable cassette player from home. 'Put a tape on, Becs!' It was very hard to hear any of the music above the noise of the car, but it was better than nothing. Suki decided to keep her mouth shut till they reached Nain's.

Eventually, the car turned down the road for Rhos. It was late evening and the grass in the hedgerows was long and clouds of gnats hovered around the bushes. Just outside the village, next to the new house, Ty'n Llidiart, were the remains of some concrete huts.

'See that, Bec,' Rhys gestured to the empty field, 'Prisoner of War camp that was.'

'Really?' Beca leant out of the window, lifting her sunglasses off her eyes, and Rhys slowed the car to a crawl. It was not very impressive, the odd doorway just visible, but no walls higher than hip height, and anyway Nia and Suki had seen it all before.

'Iola Mary says it was a holiday camp.'

'Yes, Ni, well that was after, wasn't it, stupid?'

'Doesn't look very secure, though does it? I mean, was there a wall or barbed wire or something?' Beca replaced her shades.

'Well there wasn't exactly anywhere for them to go, was there?' answered Rhys, 'And anyway, they were all doing farm work, so they had to come and go, didn't they? Some of them even lived out on the farms.'

Beca shuddered. 'I wouldn't have fancied that, all those Nazis wandering about.'

'Not all Germans were Nazis, you know.' Suki spoke for the first time since Penmaen-mawr, 'and some were Italian, too, and anyway, they weren't all bad. Nain said her and Mrs Davies used to fancy some of them.'

Beca was still not convinced. 'But it was different then. They were on the other side, weren't they? They were the enemy! I wouldn't have liked living next to a place like that. They could have escaped or something, and murdered everyone!'

Nia had stopped listening. Beyond the old buildings, in the adjoining field, she had seen a pony. There didn't used to be any ponies in Rhos. Oh, the Bowens towards Nefyn kept Cobs, but they were for showing, in hand usually, and not for riding. And the Bowens always seemed altogether too grand to ask if she could help out.

Nia looked harder. The pony was chestnut, 13 maybe 14 hands. It looked Araby but it was hard to tell. That field belonged to Ty'n Llidiart—she could just see the top of the house, well hidden by bushes and set back from the road.

The car began to speed up. 'Hang on, Rhys! Wait just a minute!' She didn't want to shout, 'Look, a pony!' as she knew the others would think she was about six. So she said nothing, and Rhys drove on into the village, past the playing field and the big white house that used to be the doctor's, past the Howell's shop and up the hill to Nain's.

The car struggled up the hill to Acre Uchaf. The road was very narrow and the high-sided hedges brushed the side of the car. 'Becs,' Rhys's voice was low, and the two girls in the back seat instinctively pricked up their ears. 'Don't be scared of Heulwen Haf, she's all right.'

Suki was indignant. 'Of course she's all right, Rhys! She's your aunt, isn't she?'

The farm, well it was just a smallholding really, was on the top of a hill. On a clear day you could just about see the sea on both sides. In a storm, the wind was enough to blow you off your feet and the flares from boats in trouble on the sea lit up the sky like a firework display. The farmhouse itself was a modern bungalow, built about ten years ago when the roof of the old house blew off. There was the usual collection of farm buildings, and the rusting six-berth caravan in the yard, where the Robertses and Josephs had come for the school holidays over the years.

Most of the land had been sold off, leaving three

fields, a handful of sheep and some chickens. It was Taid's hobby really. In the bottom field, Cae Llan, stood a smart, sleek modern caravan which was let out from April to September and provided a good portion of Mr and Mrs Gruffudd's income.

As they turned into the yard Nain and Heulwen Haf came out to meet them. Monica Rose, her gummy-eyed old sheep dog was skulking about, growling out of the corner of her mouth. Heulwen, pleased to see them but shy and wary of Beca, smiled, but kept her eyes on the floor. Nain hugged them all and shook hands with Beca, discreetly eyeing her up and down, then shooed them into the kitchen where Taid was already sitting at the table carving the meat.

Suki groaned. 'Oh, Nain, didn't Mum tell you I'm a vegetarian?'

6

The following morning was unusually bright, with blue skies and only a few tiny non-threatening clouds. Nia was awake first, used to being up and down at the stables even before her mother had returned from the nightshift. She looked at the clock. It was still only seven. Suki would be asleep for ages and the morning looked too good to miss. If she took one of the bikes she could ride down to Ty'n Llidiart and have a good look at the chestnut pony she'd seen yesterday, and be back for breakfast.

She went out to the barn and had a look at the bikes. There were a couple of rusting old hulks that looked totally unridable, Rhys's old racing bike that was just about usable, except that none of the gears worked and the chain kept coming off, a girl's bike, with a basket, which was far too small and had no brakes, and on the opposite wall, well apart from the others, Nia smiled to herself, as though she'd thought rust was contagious, was Suki's bike. Suki won't mind, well anyway she won't know, thought Nia, and I'll be back before she's even awake.

She quickly forgot any doubts she had about borrowing the bike. It was a joy to ride, infinitely better than Lowri's cast off she rode at home, and before she knew it, Nia was back at the old Prisoner of War camp at the side of Ty'n Llidiart. It was very quiet—an early morning stillness which was slightly eerie. The concrete ruins were sticking up like rotten stumps through the grass, a sort of miniature modern Stonehenge.

Nia hesitated before wheeling the bike in through the open gateway, then she laid it down gently on the damp grass, as if any noise might wake the new people in Ty'n Llidiart, or perhaps long gone occupants of these concrete huts. 'Don't be so daft, Nia Roberts.' She spoke it out loud, like a magic charm. Then laughed at herself for even thinking such rubbish.

She could see the pony in the far field, with another smaller, shaggier companion, and called to it, fishing in her jacket pocket for a couple of Polo mints. The chestnut lifted its head and looked up at her then walked, rangily, over to where she stood by the wire fence. The shaggy companion followed, keeping its head to the grass like a Hoover.

The chestnut was about 14 hands—'Just my size, aren't you, sausage?'—with a white blaze down his face and three white socks. Nia itched behind his ears and tickled under his chin and the pony nosed in her pockets for more Polos, stretching his neck above and over the spiky wire fence. 'No! . . . I haven't got anymore!'

Suddenly she heard the sound of a door opening, and loud pop music emptied out into the field. Both ponies looked expectantly towards the house: they knew their breakfast was coming. Nia froze. There was something very embarrassing about being discovered patting someone else's horse before nine o'clock in the morning. Okay, so she wasn't in their field, she wasn't trespassing, but she would rather introduce herself at a more opportune and decorous time.

She ducked down instinctively, even though the fence was wire, and crouched along the ground till she reached the safety of the hedge. She had a broad grin on her face, and was trying to suppress a giggling fit. If she was discovered now she would look truly silly. She tried to get round to the bike as quietly as possible.

Suki didn't wake until the sun had moved round onto her face. She stretched and lifted up a corner of the thin, tea-towelish curtains and looked out into the yard. In the bungalow opposite, she could see Heulwen Haf hoovering the sitting room. Suki caught sight of the clock. It was eight-thirty.

'Ooh, Ni! Why didn't you . . .' but she didn't finish her sentence. Nia was up and gone. Suki jumped out of bed and pulled on some clothes and slippers then headed for the house.

Half-way across the yard the smell of Taid's cooked breakfast, bacon and fried bread, came out to meet her. Just as she was ready to succumb to the delights of crispy bacon, she noticed her bike, or rather, she noticed the space where her bike had been.

Suki strode into the kitchen, 'Nia! Ni! Where is she? I told her, Nain, I told her!'

Nain was sitting at the table drinking tea and doing the crossword in the paper. 'What did you tell her, love? Sit down and have your breakfast.'

Half an hour later Nia returned, suitably apologetic, but Suki's ranting washed right over her. She had already discovered from Nain last night that the new people in Ty'n Llidiart were called Parry-Jones, and now she had called in on Sarah Howell on her way back to Acre Uchaf this morning to find out more.

'Her name's Lisa or something, the older one that is . . . She's got a sister too, Amanda-Jane. Sounds like a doll to me. Anyway, they don't mix in much, a bit too pleased with themselves and their ponies, always going on about where they used to live and what they used to do. I think she's OK though. But Iola Mary and Lisa don't get on.'

Which of course, thought Nia, was the kiss of death socially, in Rhos. 'I think,' Sarah went on, smiling, 'that they're a bit too much like each other, you know,' then in a whisper 'but Lisa is prettier! Oh, I don't mind Lisa really but I don't know anything about horses, do I? She'll probably love you.'

This, of course, was exactly what Nia had wanted to hear. 'Oh no Sarah! Is that the time? Suki will be up and I've got her bike!'

And with that Nia hared out of the shop catching the magazine rack with the corner of her jacket, sending a fountain of *Golwg* and *Cosmopolitan* up into the air and on to the floor. 'Ni!' Sarah shouted after her, but Nia was off, back up the hill, in top gear.

'So, girls!' Nain was wiping down the kitchen table and Heulwen was clearing the breakfast things. Nia was gazing out of the window wondering about Lisa Parry-Jones. Suki was glaring at her, still cross about the bike. 'Have you thought what you're going to be doing?'

Taid was filling his pipe, the *Daily Post* spread out on his lap.

'Well, I'm going to Pwllheli with Heulwen shopping, if you to want to come.' Nain was shouting from the kitchen now. 'Mind, the weather's good. You might be better off making the most of it. Take a picnic lunch down to the beach, or something.'

'No thanks, Nain,' Nia got up and headed for the back door, 'I think I'll see what the girls down the village are doing.' She hadn't exactly worked out what her strategy would be, but she knew this holiday was looking more promising already.

'Hey, Nia!' Suki got up after her, following her across the yard to the caravan. 'What about me?'

'Well, you can come too, I'm not stopping you!' But that wasn't exactly what Nia meant and Suki knew it.

Nia didn't really want to have to cope with Suki tagging along all day. It would be so much easier on her own.

'I don't want to hang around here all day!' Suki was almost whining.

Nia sighed, 'Look, I said I wasn't stopping you! What more do you want?'

'Come on, Ni, you know I don't get on with Wendy and Iola!' Suki was standing in the yard, Nia walking on towards the road.

'That's not my problem, is it?' Nia shouted back at her. 'You don't HAVE to come!'

Nia had just turned round the corner into the lane.

'OK, I'll come then, OK?' Suki ran to catch her up.

They walked in silence the quarter of a mile or so to Bryntirion, the farm where Iola lived.

'Hiya, Ni!' Iola Mary opened the back door, still in her dressing gown. 'Hiya, Suki! You two look like a wet weekend! Enjoying your holiday?'—she smiled sarcastically— 'Sarah phoned to say she'd seen you.'

In the large kitchen Iola and her younger sister Eirlys were still having breakfast. Their mother was driving Rhian, who was eighteen, to work in Abersoch where she worked at the golf club. This, according to Iola, was 'Great, 'cos she gets to meet all these dead sexy men!'

This was not of any interest at all to Nia, and Suki rolled her eyes in disgust. Eirlys giggled.

'What are you up to today then?' Nia asked, when eventually she managed to get a word in.

'Oh, I dunno. Wendy is going to Pwllheli with her Mam, shopping. I might go too. Robert Davies —do you know him?—from Fron Isa, over Tudweiliog, has a job for the holidays in the burger bar downtown.'

'I didn't know there was a downtown in Pwllheli,' said Suki quietly, but no one was taking any notice of her anyway.

'I suppose,' continued Iola, pouring herself a cup of tea, 'you've already seen the horses at Ty'n Llidiart.'

'Ponies,' corrected Nia. 'I also heard you don't like their owner much!'

'Lisa Parry-Jones!' Iola said the name in a singsong little girl voice. 'They're too stuck up for round here, that lot!'

'Well maybe,' added Suki, pointedly, 'your little gang doesn't give them a chance.'

'Only thing she's interested in is bloody horses!' Iola was dismissive.

'All the boys round here think she's great looking!

Even Wendy says she's pretty!' Eirlys piped up, smirking.

Iola turned to face her little sister, 'Only sometimes, Wendy said. *Sometimes* she looks pretty!'

Nia and Suki left, Nia promising to meet up with the others one evening in the week—she'd been invited to a dance at Botwnnog.

'She didn't ask me!' Suki was sulky.

'You wouldn't want to go anyway, would you?'

Nia was not interested in Suki's problems. She hadn't got any further with Lisa Parry-Jones and decided she would just have to go there and take her chance. But after lunch, and on her own.

7

From the other side of the road Nia could see Lisa, well she assumed it was her, brushing down the chestnut pony as it stood tied up by the side of the field shelter. The shelter was brand new, almost bright orange under several coats of creosote, with a dark green sloping roof. Lisa, if it was her, did look sort of glamorous, especially for Rhos, even in jodhs and a sweatshirt. She was slim, medium height, but that wasn't it, and her face looked reasonably ordinary. No, thought Nia, it was the red hair, shiny in a fat plait that hung almost to her waist.

Why, thought Nia, did boys always go for the really corny things? She'd seen it at school. They all went for the obvious: big bust, long legs, high heels, pointy fingernails, silly laugh, long hair. Preferably the full set, but in most cases any one of these attributes was enough. Did they have no imagination? Nia decided not, and hoping that they grew out of those sort of ideas, she took a deep breath and crossed the road.

Lisa Parry-Jones was fifteen and, as Nia suspected, was intensely proud of her hair. She had perfected a way of tossing her head when she laughed to show it off and decided that it didn't look too contrived. She washed it every other day and, of course, would never, ever cut it. She had her problems too, though; her parents, her little sister Amanda-Jane, and a podgy face. It was puppy fat really, that had almost left everywhere else but clung stubbornly to her chin and cheekbones. Sometimes after a bath on Sunday night she would sit in front of her Mum's dressing table and move her jaws around frantically or pummel herself under the chin like it said to do in all those women's magazines.

But what she had been most annoyed about was moving, being stuck here in the middle of this god-awful village, miles from anywhere. At least she had Louie. She sighed and concentrated on the pony's particularly muddy tail.

Nia, meanwhile, hadn't really thought this one out. She knew the worst Lisa Parry-Jones could do was say 'No' but she could feel her mouth getting drier. Should she knock at the front door of the house or stand at the edge of the field waving

'Cooee', like Nain does to the visitors? She decided knocking was the best option and walked up the crunchy gravel drive to the big navy blue door. A small delicate woman answered. Nia didn't know this formal looking woman. 'Are you one of Lisa's friends from the village? She's out with her pony I think. You'll find her round the back, dear, all right?' She smiled a polite little smile and shut the door. That wasn't the introduction Nia had expected but she walked round the back of the house as she'd been told.

Lisa saw her coming and looked up from her work. 'Hello, can I help?'

'Your Mum sent me round. I did knock. My name's Nia.'

Lisa started brushing again. 'I haven't seen you in Rhos before. What do you want?'

Of course Lisa knew what she wanted and she was pleased. No one in Rhos seemed to be at all interested in horses, except some of Amanda-Jane's friends and they were always asking for a ride, but she didn't want little nine year olds messing him about. In their old village, near Wrexham, girls, even from the sixth form college, fell over themselves to muck out and clean tack, to ride her horse, to be her friend. She could see them coming and here came one now. But she would make her sweat, just a bit.

'He's lovely,' ventured Nia, coming closer. Louie nosed forward, half remembering the smell of Polos from that morning and whickered at her. Lisa pulled the pony's head back towards her.

'Yes. I've had him for two years now. He's my second pony, Welsh Cross Arab.'

All Nia could manage was a lame 'Yes.'

Then there was about a minute during which the only sound was of Lisa brushing the horse, then cleaning the brush with the curry comb. Lisa could have said, 'Here, give me a hand,' but she was enjoying making Nia wait.

'Do you have your own horse?' Lisa asked, already knowing the answer. Nia knew what she was doing, the awful tyranny of the pony owner, but she went along with it all the same.

'No . . . but I help at stables and I've been riding for years . . .' She tried not to sound too desperate, 'I want to do my A.I. after school.'

Lisa could think of nothing worse than being an A.I., an Assistant Instructor, seventeen or eighteen, living in a caravan at the back of some riding school, working all hours for nothing, sometimes even paying for the privilege! 'That's nice,' she said, but didn't sound convinced. 'You don't live round here, do you?'

Nia explained how she was on holiday, with her grandparents, how boring it was, and eventually, 'I was, um, wondering, if you . . . needed any help or anything. I can clean tack or do grooming, you know, or I could lunge him if he needed exercise . . . if you were busy.'

Lisa looked up at Nia. It was like looking into the

eyes of a puppy begging to be walked. Lisa smiled. 'Can you plait up?'

'Um, yes, I won first for turnout at our show last Easter.' Nia was smiling too. It looked like she was in with a chance, and she did a running plait better than Ceri, at least.

'I could do with a groom. Usually I just get Dad, or worse, Manda! I'm entering Louie for Working Hunter Pony in Pwllheli, so you could give us a hand. Well, if you're still here.'

Nia smiled wider.

'I'd have to try you out first, of course.' Lisa tossed her Titian plait. 'You know what I mean, if you had a horse you wouldn't want just anyone riding him. Could you come back, tomorrow morning maybe?'

Nia floated back up the hill to Nain's on a cloud. All the rest of the afternoon it was Lisa this and Louie that. Suki eventually got cross and went out with Heulwen Haf to give Monica Rose her walk.

It was really sunny and Nia went to lie in the long grass in the top field, imagining poor old Lisa Parry-Jones breaking her collar-bone at the last minute and Nia, to the rescue, winning the red rosette for best Working Hunter Pony.

She was just steadying Louie in the line-up for the judging of the championship cup when Monica Rose came waddling through the dark green grass and didn't so much lick, as grunt and snuffle, right into her ear. Suki followed close behind.

'Have you been here all afternoon?' She seemed brighter.

'Maybe, what if I have?'

'You should have come with me and Heul!' Suki was smiling and slightly smug.

'I can come out with you lot and that excuse for a dog anytime!' Nia lay, eyes closed, chewing the end of a grass stem.

'Well if you're going to be like that maybe we just won't tell you!' Suki was annoyed. Nia seemed so self-contained. To be honest, she and Heul hadn't had that great a time, well nothing spectacular. It was good to be out in the air, and the hills really did look fantastic, rust red with bracken, sloping down to the sea. It made her feel good and want to be part of it again—that 'This is home' feeling. Now it felt like Nia had just burst her bubble. She turned, catching Monica Rose by the collar, and then tugged her back down the hill towards the house. Nia rolled over in the grass and bowed as the judge pinned on the 'Best in Show' rosette and took the lap of honour.

That evening Heulwen and Nain were busy, some *Merched y Wawr* treasure hunt in the next village. Nia sat hunched over 'Schooling your Horse or Pony' trying to figure out how she would wow L. P-J in the morning, hoping she wouldn't fluff it.

Suki was fidgety, flicking through *Womans' Own,* the telly turned up too loud so Taid could hear the News.

'Ni? . . .'

'Hmmm?'

'Ni, do you want a game of draughts?'

'No thanks.'

'Ni?'

'What!'

'What about hangman or consequences or something?'

'Suki!' Nia took her eyes from her book for a second. 'I'm busy!'

Suki headed back to the caravan, slamming the front door extra hard as she went. This, however, failed to register above the noise of the TV. In the dark she turned on her torch—there was no electricity in their caravan—and lay on her narrow bed, almost wanting to cry. What was Cecile doing now, she wondered. 'Here I am,' she thought, 'thirteen, reasonably pretty from some angles, and living in the heart, well on the edge, of the most exciting city in Europe, and here I am at half past nine, on my way to sleep in a poxy caravan in the middle of nowhere!' A small thudding noise, like a pebble wrapped in cotton wool, caught her attention. It was a moth with a death wish trying to meet its maker against the tiny bulb of her torch. She watched the little thing thump itself three times, then did it a kindness and flicked off the light.

'The middle of nowhere!' She said it out loud this time. Iola and Wendy often cursed Rhos as a dump and as nowhere, and often she'd defended it as part of her home.

'You, you don't know you're bloody born, you!' Iola had laughed back at her. 'I'd give anything to live in London! You couldn't really live here. You're just a visitor like all the others!'

Suki rolled over. Remembering made her feel uncomfortable.

8

The next day, Suki resolved not to waste any more time in self indulgent moping. She could have as a good a time as Nia, with a bit of effort. She would walk and do some drawings for school, and see if she could hang out with Meinir Evans, who was a bit younger than the rest of the village lot, but she'd always got on with her. This sounded a lot better than doing nothing and anyway, she didn't need Nia and her stupid ponies.

Meanwhile, Nia had been up at dawn, polishing her boots and then walking round the farmyard trying to make them look less shiny and more well used. Luckily, no one else had been up early enough to catch her, except the Smeatons, up for a day trip to Offa's Dyke, or somewhere. Nia had waved to them and tried to look as entirely normal as possible, but expected they'd thought, or rather hoped, she was in the middle of some rustic Welsh boundary-beating ceremony.

What to wear took a lot of deciding. The black jodphurs were most business-like, and a T-shirt with a collar. She had rehearsed what she would do, after spending the best part of an hour last night on the phone to Ceri in consultation. Walk and trot various circles, try and get a feel of how he went, get him balanced and on the bit. She smiled at herself for sounding like Mrs Pritchard, her riding teacher. She felt alternately ecstatic and strangled with nerves. She hoped there wouldn't be jumps. Please God, make it all go OK.

She couldn't eat any breakfast and watching Heulwen dipping buttery soldiers into a gloopy egg yolk made her feel greener than ever. She checked the time: the clock hands seemed to be made of lead they moved so slowly. It was still only nine. Another hour to go, at least. She didn't want to appear too keen.

Suki seemed suspiciously jolly, and that didn't help either. Curiosity eventually got the better of Nia. 'Are you up to something?'

'Me? No!' Suki answered through a mouthful of toast.

'Well, you'd better keep out of my way this morning.' Nia was almost snarling.

'Oh!' Suki replied in mock surprise. 'Me and Heul were going to bring Monica Rose down to Ty'n Llidiart to watch you fall off your horse!'

Nia did not smile.

'I was only joking, Ni.' But Nia had already left the table. 'Oh well, suit yourself!'

Nia walked very slowly down to Lisa's, breathing deeply and hoping she had used enough deodorant. The sun was beginning to warm up, and the last thing she wanted was dripping armpits. Even so, she still managed to be a bit too early for comfort so she hung around by the side of the field, feeding Louie Polos in the hope the pony would feel like doing her a few favours in return.

Lisa appeared noiselessly, making Nia jump almost out of her skin. Lisa had a bright blue headcollar for Louie that almost squeaked with newness. As she slipped it over the pony's head Nia noticed a thick red-gold bangle that slid down Lisa's arm.

'Ooh! That's lovely!' Nia hadn't meant to say anything.

'Yes,' Lisa smiled. 'It matches Louie.' Nia was still gawping. 'And me!' Lisa laughed, rather weakly, at her own joke.

Secretly, Lisa was hoping her Mother hadn't seen her put it on. It was really only for very special occasions, a present from when she had been Aunt Katy's bridesmaid last summer. But this was a bit of an occasion, she had told herself. It was impress the yokels time. And this yokel was about to be impressed.

But when Nia dismounted, some fifteen minutes later, it was Lisa who was impressed. In fact, if anything, she was jealous that Louie seemed to go so well for Nia.

'Oh, well done!' This was Nia talking to the pony, patting him enthusiastically on his neck, then tickling his mane 'Oh, Lisa! you are lucky!'

Lisa didn't want to give too much away. She was thinking that if Nia schooled him like that every day she'd have no problem at Pwllheli next month.

'You did well,' Lisa conceded. 'Nia, isn't it?' Nia

smiled gratefully at her. 'Tell you what,' Lisa added, 'Why don't you stick around and give me a hand this morning, and this afternoon, if you like. I was going to build a little course.'

Nia nodded almost frantically. Ceri was not going to believe this at all.

Suki was trying not to feel cross at being abandoned. She would ignore Nia, well that was the idea, but riding her bike over towards the cluster of curiously white council houses on the far side of Rhos, Suki was constantly reminded of her.

It was impossible to walk or cycle around the village without being waved at or Yoo-hooed by practically every old lady in sight. 'Hello, dear, how is your Mother these days? Hmm? Keeping well, I hope, and where is Nia?' This was a pattern repeated at least six or seven times before she reached Meinir's.

Most of the time Suki could only manage a vague recollection as to who these old biddies were but she always remembered Mrs Rose, who had three hairs growing out of a mole on her chin and who, without fail, would press one or two yucky mint imperials into her hand before she could get away.

Meinir's family, the Evanses, were like one of those families in some TV soap, Suki thought. There were five children—Geraint, Anwen, Harri, Meinir, and Iolo who was only one. Their parents were constantly rowing. Big rows. Broken windows, Mrs Evans leaving for the Isle of Man with her lover from Llangefni, Mr Evans throwing all her clothes out of the bedroom window into the street and changing the locks.

But that had been before Iolo had been born. Something mysterious had happened. Now they were like newly weds, holding hands as they walked to the post office to pick up the family credit, kissing at the bus stop and going on second and third honeymoons, leaving little Iolo in the capable hands of Anwen or Harri. (Geraint worked in Birmingham and sent money back when he could).

The older children seemed to take it all in their stride and were without exception, kind, unbitchy and hardworking. To some in Rhos, it seemed unfair that two fiery and volatile parents should produce such well-adjusted children.

Suki was by now ringing the ding-dong-Avon-calling doorbell of Meinir's house. She seemed to have been waiting for ever and was just about to head off when Harri opened the door. He was tall for sixteen and prettier than Meinir, but his too-long fringe was always in his eyes and Iolo, wriggling nappy-less in his big brothers arms, was depositing two green tusks of baby snot on Harri's chest.

Suki thought he was vaguely fanciable, but she knew that Iola and Wendy were after him. That and the baby snot were enough to put her off.

'Mei's at Iola's with Eirlys, I think.' His voice was a monosyllabic grunt, common to most adolescent boys, which involved practically no upper lip movement at all. You could smile at least, Suki said to herself, but all that came out was 'Oh, thanks.'

Then there was at least two minutes of silence while neither could think of anything else to say. It was excruciating. Eventually Suki managed a feeble 'Gosh, Iolo's grown!', said her goodbye and comforted herself with the thought that she couldn't be witty and devastating one hundred per cent of the time.

Suki didn't fancy sitting in some old barn while Iola held court smoking smelly cigarettes and dispensing useless information about boys. And as she wheeled her bike back up the hill again she looked at the Garn, rising up at the back of the village, sunlit and inviting.

9

Later that evening, Nia had not come back. She did phone to tell Nain she was having supper with the Parry-Joneses, and the only one who was in any way concerned was Suki. Half jealous, half annoyed and very fidgety, unable to sit still, she seemed unable to settle to anything. She was beginning to feel left out already. Eventually, she agreed to a game of draughts with Heulwen Haf, who won easily, as usual. Then she said her 'Goodnights' and headed for the caravan.

She crossed the yard, the lights of the house throwing huge shapes out over the fields. Over in Cae Llan she could hear the Smeatons hooting over the remains of their barbecue. She paused, looking out towards the dark black sea. It was so dark here, no lights at all, no time to be walking about. Anything could happen. She remembered her feeble attempt that afternoon to go up the Garn. In broad daylight.

She had been about half an hour out of the village, just on the lower slopes of the Garn, when she stopped, admiring the view down to the nose of Llŷn. The sky was almost clear, and the only sounds were sheep calling and a few birds twittering. It was beautiful. There were no other walkers up that side of the mountain this afternoon.

There were no other walkers. She hadn't thought about that before and suddenly she was scared, very very scared. In London, if you thought someone was after you you could knock on a door or go into a shop. You were never really alone. But here there was no house, no shop, no people, not one. No one would hear her, no one to ask for help.

Instantly her country walk had become a mad dash back down the mountain. Full pelt, hurtling downwards, running, almost falling, through the bracken, until she stood in the yard at Acre Uchaf, heart still pounding, pretending nothing had happened. London, she decided, was infinitely safer than this.

As she got into bed Suki heard the rattle of Ni's bike and the crash as she tried leaning it up against the house, then letting it fall onto the stone step by the kitchen door. There was a shouted hello to Nain and the sound of Nia's booted feet stomping towards the caravan.

Nia was about as ecstatic as she could get. She threw herself heavily onto the bed, tired but more talkative than she had been for days. 'Oh, Suki, it's great, I can go every morning and clean the shelter and get him ready and, this is the best bit, I get half an hour on my own to school him! Hah! Ceri won't believe it! Neither do I! And she's so nice really and her family is lovely!'

Suki sat up in bed, angry with Nia for being so happy. 'Glad you came, then, Ni?'

But Nia couldn't hear the edge in her voice, and flopped into bed, too excited and exhausted to care. She slept like a log, dreaming her Dad had won the pools and come home. Only it wasn't home. It was Ty'n Llidiart. And her Mum had a perm and was glamorous in an old lady way and Rhys was neat and tidy and there was a pony and a stable and Mum and Dad bought her anything she wanted. She didn't want to wake up.

The next morning over breakfast, Nia asked Suki to Ty'n Llidiart, but Suki was dismissive.

'And what would I do? Watch while you and that Lisa ponce about with some poor dumb animal, shoving half a ton of metal in its mouth, and beating it up with a stick? No thanks!'

She had her 'Fight Factory Farming NOW!' T-shirt on.

Nia did not bother arguing. 'You just don't understand at all.' It was an adult exasperation.

Nia was full of the pony and the people at Ty'n Llidiart and their brand new Range Rover and about the show and how Lisa Parry-Jones had two saddles!

'Has she got two bottoms then?' Suki asked sarcastically.

Heulwen giggled, her hand in front of her mouth. She didn't speak that much English but she knew bottom was rude. Nain started on Suki for being unpleasant.

Lisa had agreed to let Nia give her a lesson on the lunge. Nia seemed much more grown up in control of the pony, giving instructions, but Lisa wouldn't concentrate, and eventually Nia had to give up. 'I can't help it, Ni,' Lisa giggled. 'I just can't! Let's go out for a hack before lunch.'

Nia's face read there-is-more-to-riding-than-galloping-about, but she started winding up the lunge line anyway.

Suki had been sent to the little shop for the paper and Taid's truly awful pipe tobacco, 'Y *Bwthyn',* smellable up to a distance of three miles. Sarah Howell was serving, well sitting reading *Just Seventeen* and drinking tea. She was small and not quite skinny, with brown hair beginning to grow out of a bob. As she spoke she twirled a little bit of hair, next to her right ear, around in her fingers. She offered Suki some tea, but Suki declined. 'I'm too busy being bored!'

Sarah looked up from the problem page. 'Where's Ni then?'

As she spoke, Lisa and Nia, on pony and bicycle,

passed the shop window. Sarah saw the look on Suki's face, 'You know, Iola Mary doesn't like her either. I think she's OK, though.'

Suki smiled. 'That must be the first thing that me and Iola agree on then!'

As Suki was leaving, Sarah told her about the dance. Suki made her excuses, but Sarah wouldn't have it. 'Oh, go on, you said you were bored, now you've got something to look forward to!'

'Some poky old village disco!' Suki was utterly dismissive, then realised she had opened her mouth and fallen right in. Again.

Sarah giggled, 'You don't do yourself any favours, do you?' Suki was humbled. Sarah continued, 'OK, Miss Uptown Sophistication, this may be the sticks as far as you're concerned, and Botwnnog School Hall may not be London by night, but it is a laugh!'

'Oh Sarah, I'm sorry, really. I'll think about it.'

Suki stopped on her way out, to study the photocopied poster on the door. It was blackened and smudgy, with the Urdd logo hand-coloured with felt pen. Next Friday, a week tomorrow, Under Eighteens (Suki groaned) disco, Botwnnog School Hall, Botwnnog. Sarah smiled at her through the glass as the door tinkled and shut. Suki walked slowly back up the hill to Nain's, alternately deciding that on no account would she go, then pondering what she would wear if she decided to change her mind.

Suki sat on the edge of her mattress in the caravan half trying to read a book, half staring out at the landscape sloping treeless towards the sea. She could see into the kitchen too—Nain fussing round Heulwen, getting her ready to go out. Heulwen was oblivious, as usual.

10

Heulwen Haf was 48 going on 7½. She moved and ate like a bird. She looked a bit like one too, all small, sharp, pointy features, hair drawn back under a headscarf, like the Queen. She could talk, though often only via Nain and never to strangers. She spent most of her time as Nain's shadow, standing close by her when they were out, or sitting quietly in the corner of the room in which she was working. Or out on long walks mumbling to herself or Monica Rose, her livery-brown and white old sheepdog.

She was not totally gaga, she knew and understood a lot more than she gave away. It was her way of hiding and staying cut off from the world. Sometimes she would sing loudly for no reason or laugh uncontrollably, as she walked down to the shop, hugging herself close to the hedgerow at the side of the road. Sometimes she would weep, inconsolably, sitting in her chair nearest the telly, in front of *Through the Keyhole* or *Home and Away,* rocking, and stroking Monica Rose rhythmically. Or, at night, you'd hear her sobbing or moaning in her bedroom, a bit like Mrs Rochester in *Jane Eyre,* Suki thought.

But Heulwen Haf had been born this way. Her mental state had not come about through unrequited love, or mistreatment. Aunty Ceinwen, who as a nurse was consulted on all family medical matters, said it was probably lack of oxygen when she had been born, that or some kind of in-built autism. 'It was difficult with twin births in those days.' Anyway whatever it was, no one was frightened of Heulwen Haf, well, only little kids who didn't know her, or didn't know any better. It seemed more than a little unfair that Dilys was so clever, so achieving, and Heulwen, her twin, just a few minutes younger, seemed to be on another planet.

Heulwen Haf and Suki had always been special friends. Maybe it was because Suki was the youngest, or that she was Dilys's. Or because Suki didn't fit in so well with the village kids, or because Heulwen Haf didn't mind listening to Suki's pidgin Welsh. 'If you're twins, Mum,' Suki had asked, 'why don't you look more alike?' They were both smallish and dark, but Dilys was more like Nain, and Heulwen, well, Heulwen was just Heulwen.

'Well, love, there's identical and non-identical, isn't there.' Her mother was always a bit touchy on the subject. Deep down her mother seemed guilty, and Suki thought sometimes it might be just as hard being the 'normal' one.

Anyway, Nain had fetched Heul's anorak and favourite bag, a shopping bag with a picture of Prince Charles and Princess Diana. Then Nain waved her off and Suki had jumped out of the caravan to catch her up.

'Heul! ... Heulwen! Hang on!' Heulwen Haf clutched her bag tighter. 'It's only me! Suki!'

Heulwen smiled

'Can I come with you? Where are you going?'

Heulwen at last stopped walking and opened her bag for Suki to inspect. Suki craned forward for a better look.

'Oh!'

It was about a week's worth of old carrot tops and cabbage leaves.

Heulwen smiled. 'For Sandy Gall!'

Suki was puzzled.

Heulwen smiled wider, 'Sandy Gall, Cornwal Isa!'

Suki smiled too, 'Oh, your cow, er, no, bull!'

'Bullock!' Heulwen corrected.

'Of course!'

Sandy Gall had been born in the spring and had two huge black eyes and two double jointed black velvet ears. It had been love at first sight. Even Monica Rose was jealous, but Heulwen always did like cows. And Taid had stopped keeping cattle since Isla St Clair, a big soppy Friesian, had died a few years ago.

Sandy Gall lived at Cornwal Isa, a few miles away. Suki knew all about him by the time they reached the lane up to the house. Suki knew a bit about Cornwal Isa too. It was owned by the Lewises, a big old farming family that ran several farms in the area. Taid used to work on and off for them, extra work in the summer, or spring, that sort of thing. She also knew that Mrs Myfi Lewis, who was very formidable but handsome in an old ladyish sort of way, liked to think of Heulwen as another 'good work', like the one day a week she did in the charity shop in Pwllheli. She also remembered her Mum telling her that once, in the dim and distant past, Gwilym, the eldest boy, had had a desperate crush on her.

It was a beautiful house, exactly symmetrical, like an unblinking open face. Suki could have stood in front of it for hours imagining it was hers, but Heulwen had already begun to drag her round to the outbuildings that straggled up the side of the hill behind the farmhouse. A row of oil drums at the side of the track exploded into barking and clanking. Suki nearly jumped out of her skin as a collection of shaggy sheepdogs ran out towards them as far as their chains would allow. There didn't seem to be anyone about.

'Are you sure it's OK?' Suki stayed close to Heulwen's side.

The back door of the farmhouse opened and there was Mrs Lewis beaming broadly and pulling on a pair of wellingtons and an overall.

'Heulwen! You're early! And this is Dilys's girl! Lovely!' Suki smiled weakly. 'Your Nain tells me you're as clever as your Mother!'

'Um. Thank you.'

Heulwen was nodding and smiling and thankfully, as far as Suki was concerned, more interested in seeing to Sandy than making small talk.

The Lewis herd of Welsh Black cattle was envied and reasonably famous. Suki could see some of them in the nearest field, all shaggy black with primeval pointy horns. Sandy would win prizes: his real name was something like Prince something something of Uwchmynydd.

Mrs Lewis asked them in for tea. Inside the kitchen gleamed with snow white newness. Suki was disappointed. She had been hoping for a black cooking range and 'interesting' furniture. They drank tea and ate bread and butter.

'Your Auntie Heulwen is entering Sandy for us at Pwllheli! That's nice!'

She was smiling and loud as if Heulwen was deaf as well as everything else. Suki smiled. She meant well at least.

Suki fidgeted. She could see into the hall, running dark and windowless to the obviously rarely used front door. She could see pictures.

'May I have a look?'

The air was still and smelt stale and she could hear the grandfather clock near the door working itself up to chime. All along the walls, pictures and little plaques glinted in the gloom. It was all cattle, some chap in a cap or a hat with a number round his waist dwarfed by one of the strange archaic-looking animals the stamp of those she'd seen outside.

Suddenly she felt Mrs Lewis and Heulwen right beside her. 'They're, um, very nice,' and she really did mean it even though it didn't sound quite right. It was like looking at another world.

Heulwen was all for getting home. It would be *Blockbusters* in half an hour, and then *Home and Away*. She went to say goodbye to Sandy then she and Suki walked home. Mrs Lewis stood at the back door and waved them off.

'Do come another time Suki, and bring Nia! And do remember me to your mother!'

'Well then, Suki!' Nain was sewing a pair of Heulwen's tights. 'Did you have a nice time?'

'Spose so.'

Nain sighed, loudly. 'Is Nia back?'

Nia was not back and would not be back till late. Nain knew what she was thinking.

'There's that disco on Friday. That'll be fun!'

'Disco! Oh, Nain!' Suki rolled her eyes. 'Nobody says Disco!'

Nain shrugged.

Suki sighed and crossed the yard to the caravan. It would be light for at least a couple more hours and she was bored stiff.

'A week! Only a week!' She said it out loud to herself then fished down the side of her bag for a book.

Every day seemed like one day less, that was all as far as Suki was concerned. What was worse was having Nia so radiantly happy. It felt a bit like looking in one of those distorting mirrors.

As for the dance, it was both exciting and terrifying. Suki had been to one party with dim lights and dancing and a few boys. But opportunities were limited for an only child at an all girls school. She knew that as a Londoner she was expected to know it all, and sometimes, she reflected, she did. But she had never really done anything.

When at last it was Friday, Nia came home at lunchtime, breezy and pink-cheeked. She stuck her head round the kitchen door.

'Hiya! I've just come for my stuff! Lisa says I can get ready at her place!'

She had almost made it to the caravan when Nain shouted 'Nia!' It was a stop-you-dead shout that Nia would've heard from Ty'n Llidiart 'Nia Roberts! I want a word!' Nain took Nia round to the front door of the house and Suki could just about hear them. There were several protests like 'Oh, Nain!' and 'Do I have to!' and Suki was just going through to the hall to get a better listen when she heard Nia stomping towards her, eyes blazing.

'It's all your fault!' Nia hissed at her so Nain couldn't hear.

Suki was cross to tears. 'It's your bloody friends and your bloody dance! I don't want to go anyway! Do what you bloody like!'

This was too much for Nain. After Suki had stormed out sobbing to the caravan, she sat Nia down, quietly this time. Nia knew in her heart it wasn't fair, she knew Nain was right, and she knew she owed Suki some time at least. But did it have to be today? Nain was adamant.

'Nia, you go and make it up to Suki, you be extra nice to her! She's farther away from home and she's younger than you, a lot younger than you, if you only knew it!'

'Only a year, Nain!'

'That's not what I meant!'

Nia squirmed in her chair.

'And no sulkiness either, mind! Now phone that Lisa up and tell her you'll see her later!'

Nia sat there after Nain had gone out to Suki. Why should Nain tell her how to feel? She couldn't just turn on and off like a tap! Nia sighed. There was no getting round it though, Nain was worse than Mum. If she stayed cross Nain would get worse. Bloody Suki.

11

After tea Suki sat in front of the telly listening to the whoosh from the water heater as Nia ran her bath. She got up and walked over to the mirror over the fireplace, untied the elastic which had almost grown into her woolly hair, and shook her hair free. Until a few years ago it had always been cut short. Now it was up to her, she had grown it into a wild tangled froth, tamed only occasionally with an application of coconut oil.

She had been introduced to the calming effects of coconut oil by Cecile, who had guided her through the range of Afro hair care products on sale in the chemist in the broadway. She had often stood in front of the shelves, reading the fantastic names and wondering what they were for, until some diligent shop assistant offered unwanted help. 'Sta-Sof-Fro', 'Aficare, no-lye conditioner' 'Total Curl Control', and her favourite, 'Bumphree, for an end to razor bumps'.

Anyway, the hair, it was too independent to be hers, stood out in wild ringlets at all angles. She tipped her head this way, then that, trying to get the curls to arrange themselves in some interesting or glamorous new way. Suddenly she thought she heard Nain coming in from the kitchen and quickly scooped the hair back into the safety of the elastic before anyone came.

Nia emerged from her bath, pale pink and steamy.

'You can have the bathroom now, Suks, I've finished.'

'It's OK, I'm not having a bath now. I haven't decided if I'm going anyway.'

'Oh, come on, Suki, it'll be fun!'

Suki didn't look convinced.

'You'll know as many people as I will!'

'Yeah, but I bet I'll be the only black person there, won't I?'

'God, Suki! You're not still on about that?' Nia sat down next to her on the sofa. 'Look I don't even think of you as "Black", none of our friends here do! Only people who don't know you.'

Suki turned to her, open mouthed. 'Well maybe that's just the problem then, isn't it?'

Nia sighed an exasperated sigh. She was used to Suki being fragile and was feeling kind. 'Did I say the wrong thing? Oh, Suki.' She leaned forward to meet Suki's gaze. 'I don't know what to say. I don't know what you want. I don't think, "My black cousin", I just think "My cousin".'

Suki said nothing.

'Look, I'm going to get dressed. I'm sorry. OK?' Nia stopped in the doorway. 'Look, Suki, if you want some sort of label, tell us all in advance. I know you're different, you feel different, but don't tell me we're still not a lot the same. And don't tell me you don't want to go tonight.'

Suki sat with her knees up to her chin and said nothing.

'Come on, Suks.'

Suki looked at her and smiled—a little, anyway. 'Why not then, Ni? OK.'

Later, in the cramped caravan, Nia began getting ready. She hunched over Taid's shaving mirror, sitting by the big end window, and examined her face. Luckily the freckles outnumbered the spots and she could go easy on the concealer stick. She wished she had a better selection of make-up. She hardly wore it, unlike some of the girls in her year at school, or Iola Mary and Wendy.

Suki tried to affect complete disinterest and lounged on her bed reading a book, eating chocolate, trying very hard to be as cool and detached as possible. Inside her head she was trying to figure out what to wear and whether or not Nia would lend her any of her make-up, especially as Suki had just given her a lecture about how discos are meat markets and you shouldn't dress for boys. Nia gave up trying to explain that she just wanted to dress up.

'I can't wear any of this stuff!' Nia wailed, almost hopelessly.

'I thought tight jodhpurs and riding boots were supposed to be sexy,' Suki replied through a mouth full of chocolate.

'Shut up, stupid!' Nia threw a pillow at her. 'So what are you wearing then, hmm?'

Suki took no notice.

'I suppose, you just happened to pack something new or expensive or both!'

'Look, if you want to borrow anything of mine, I don't mind! Go on!' Suki gestured towards her bags, mostly still unpacked on the floor.

'Oh yeah! And where am I supposed to put the extra bits of my bum which won't fit in?'

'I've got tops! Baggy ones!'

'Thanks a bunch!' Nia sat down heavily on her bed, pulling the biggest of Suki's holdalls towards her. Suki's clothes were a source of fascination, even though Nia wouldn't be seen dead in a lot of them. She had so many, and none of them had that washed-a-thousand-times look. And none of them were hand-me-downs.

'Come on, Ni, let's sort you out!' Suki peeled herself off the bed and began rummaging in a bag. 'What about this then?' She pulled out a hugely floppy T-shirt.

'I don't want to look like a tent, Suks!'

'Shorts?'
'They wouldn't fit!'
'No, these are loose on me!'
'Don't like the colour!'
'Picky, picky! Dress? Look!'
'Since when did you wear dresses?'
'From about when you did!'
'Yeah, OK, chuck it over!'

Suki threw the dress over to Nia. It was shortish but loose and swirly, dead plain. It was cornflower blue and looked nothingy, but when you put it on it sort of moved and floated.

'Ooh, I like this!'
'It's a trapeze dress.'
'Do I have to hang upside down in it then?'
'No! It's my chapel-and-tea-with-Aunty-Alys frock.' Suki was dismissive. She looked at Nia then popped another couple of squares of chocolate into her mouth. 'Suits you!'

Nia grinned. It did look good. Nia loved it, and the dress loved her. 'Thanks, Suki! Really, thanks! I'll just go in the house and show Nain!'

Suki watched out of the caravan window to make sure she'd gone and took off the shorts she was wearing, a pair of old cut down jeans. Another inch should just about do it, she said to herself. The trouble was, every time she did one leg it ended up shorter than the other and then she had to 'even it up'. By the time she'd finished they were a good deal shorter than she had meant, and together with the top she'd chosen, a stripy all-in-one job that did up between her legs, the overall effect was to say the least dodgy.

She stood in front of the half length mirror on the caravan wardrobe door and imagined Cecile was there with her. Cecile tut-tutted disprovingly, 'No way, Suks! I mean, those shorts and that tight top, jailbait or what!'

'You're worse than my mother!' but she had to agree, and settled for one of Taid's shirts over the top to cover herself up.

Her new-last-month trainers finished it off. She looked at herself again, but all you could see was shirt and trainers, so she knotted it at the waist like they do in magazines, had a go with Nia's mascara, and braved the house.

Inside she could hear Nain and Heulwen, 'Oh, Nia Roberts! There's *del*!' Nia smiled gratefully, even though *del* was not the look she had been aiming for.

'Well, Suki!' Nain had just seen her. 'You could have tried! Tell you what, sit down here and I'll do your hair!'

'Nain!'

'What?'

'It's supposed to be like this!'

'Well, well! You look like Vera Ellen on a windy day!' Nobody apart from Nain had any idea what that meant, but the girls smiled and promised to be good. Heulwen Haf grinned up at Nia from her comfy chair, stroking Nia's blue-clad arm enviously.

12

It was in the local secondary school gym. Outside, older boys revved their motorbikes, or rode up and down, showing off. The few who had cars were having their own little parties complete with loud music and cans of beer. Taid dropped them off reminding them to be good and that he would be picking them up at quarter past ten, no buts. Suki began to wish her shorts were at least an inch longer, and that she was at least seventeen, and knew how to carry-on at these sort of dos.

Suki linked arms with Nia and together they made it across the road. She was aware of Nia looking everywhere for someone she knew. Suki just concentrated on the ground in front of her toes.

'Hiya! Wen!' Nia started waving. It was Wendy, looking mature, confident, and relaxed, blowing little puffs of cigarette smoke into the air, as if to emphasize her cool.

'Are you coming in, Wend!'

Wendy shook her head, 'I'm waiting for someone!'

'What, Meinir's brother?'

Wendy's face instantly lost its composure. 'Who told you?'

Nia was smiling mischievously. 'Come on, Wen, it's common knowledge. Sarah told me you and Io had a bet on who could get him first, poor boy!'

Wendy smiled coldly back. 'No contest!'

Nia didn't really care about what was going on or what little games were being played, she felt on top of the world. It was a nothing-can-stop-me feeling that doesn't come around very often. It was partly being able to go and school Louie every morning and knowing she was actually not at all bad at riding, well, better than Lisa P-J, and partly the blue dress. She felt good, she looked good, and she was going to have a dance and go home happy.

Unfortunately this did not rub off on Suki. Suki stood awkwardly in order to hide her too-short shorts. She couldn't keep up with the stream of Welsh and resorted to nods and lame smiles. Nia introduced her to the incandescent Lisa, who flashed her straight polished teeth and then went off with Nia and two boys whom Suki sort of recognised. So much for the ultra cool home girl from the big city.

After about fifteen minutes of screwing up her eyes through the dim light, trying to see anyone she recognised, going to the toilet twice for something to do, watching the dancing and listening to awful rock music, Suki headed outside. This was not a good idea.

Inside was darker than outside, and outside were mostly older kids, mostly those who resented not being allowed to take their cigs or cans of beer into the hall. They could hear the music well enough out in the twilight, and stood about in little knots by their cars or bikes, until they headed off for the pubs in town. Suki leant against a wall by the fire exit and untied the shirt so it fell loose, then slid down the wall. She sat with her knees at her chest in a little ball.

She was just about to start feeling terribly sorry for herself, and utterly abandoned, when she heard a scuffling noise from behind the huge school dustbins. It seemed someone was trying to squeeze behind them. Aware this might be some canoodling couple, Suki first took no notice, but when she did look she saw only one pair of once-white trainers in the gap by the bin's wheels.

Suki couldn't make out what he was up to. It was a he, or a very large footed she. Peeing? No he'd have done it by now. Chucking up? Possibly. Taking some strange and dangerous drug? Unlikely. Crying, as his girlfriend had just packed him in? Maybe . . . no. What then? Eventually Suki had run out of her invented answers, and, curiosity getting the better of her, she thought she'd have a closer look.

'Harri! What are you doing?' Suki was grinning broadly. Harri was squashed in between the bins, trying to pretend he wasn't there. Someone was even more stupid than she was.

'Ssh!!' The Sssh was totally unnecessary as the music was so loud. 'It's those women!' Harri feigned mock terror, 'They're after me!'

'What Wendy and Iola?'

'And Sarah!'

'The three witches! You should be flattered!'

'Flattened, more like!' For a moment he was serious. 'Look, you won't tell them?'

'Course not!'

He was just about to squeeze out when Nia came around the corner.

'Oh there you are! I've been looking everywhere!'

'Oh, so I should have stayed propping up a table inside, while you gallivant off with Lisa Whatsit-Jones?'

'Oh don't moan, Suki!' Nia was too happy to care. 'Look, tell Taid I'll be home later!'

Suki was open mouthed. 'When later?'

'They'll drop me off!'

'Who?'

'Jonathan and Ieuan. They're taking us for a drive. They're Lisa's friends! They've got one of those jeep things—look that yellow one!' Nia waved a big wave over to the other side of the road.

Suki was genuinely shocked. 'Oh, Nia! You can't! Not without phoning or something!'

'It'll be OK, I'm with Lisa!'

'Oh, come off it, Ni. Nain and Taid'll hit the roof!'

But Nia had already gone, and Suki was left staring open-mouthed, as her cousin jumped into the back of the open-topped jeep, next to Lisa, and then was whisked away down the road towards Abersoch. She thought she would cry, until she realised someone was standing next to her, Harri, out from behind the bins.

'Well, well!' He shook his head reprovingly. 'I didn't know your Nia was in with that crowd!'

'Neither did I!' Suki was still numb, but composed now. 'They'll kill her!'

'Jonathan and Ieuan aren't that bad!'

'No! Nain and Taid, stupid!' Suki was livid. 'They'll kill me for letting her go! Bloody Nia!'

'She's looking good, your Nia!' Harri was watching the yellow jeep disappear.

'Have you got a car?' Suki sounded desperate.

Harri laughed at her, 'Me? For a start I'm only sixteen . . .'

'Well I didn't know! Oh, I wish I'd never come!' Senselessly Suki started walking after the jeep.

'Where are you going, you idiot?' Harri trotted after her only just managing to pull her clear of a car coming the other way.

'Oh! I don't know!' The sleeves of her shirt hung empty down over her hands. She looked like a four year old in dressing up clothes.

'Well, I don't see you've got anything to worry about! It's not like you were looking after Nia.'

Suki resented the implication that Nia was looking after *her*, but said nothing. She went and sat on the low wall outside the hall and smeared sooty mascara all over her face as she wiped her almost crying eyes.

Harri was right, of course. Nia would get the earache from Nain, not her. Harri sat down next to her, a mildly concerned look on his face. Suki sniffed.

'Look, I'm going back to Rhos now, walking. I've had enough. You can come if you like. We'll be back in half an hour.'

Suki searched up her sleeve for her watch. Taid wasn't picking them up until half past ten, and that meant an hour to kill before then.

'OK, Harri, I'm coming.'

They set off out of the village, Suki taking two

steps for every one of Harri's. It was just getting dim and bats dived between the tall hedgerows.

'How long will it take now?' She was beginning to whine, but her legs were getting cold and they were crossing a field now and the grass was damp. Suki could feel it would be through her trainers any minute.

'Ooh, another fifteen minutes, give or take!' He didn't even look round, and Suki was flagging.

'Can't you slow down, just a bit!'

This was not how she had envisaged her big night out. She stopped for a moment to draw breath and gazed down at the village. Little lights winked in houses, everything smelled of damp and green.

'Come on!' Harri was waiting for her at the bottom of the ridge. Suki ran to catch up, the ends of the shirt flapping down to her knees. 'You look like a long-armed ghost in that shirt!'

Suki didn't want to be scared, even a little bit. 'Shut up, Harri!'

They walked in silence as far as the edge of the village and the brand new reflecting 'Rhos' sign.

'Will Nia be all right?'

'Course! Though I wouldn't fancy snogging Ieuan or Jon!'

'Shut up, Harri!' Suki didn't want to think of it at all.

Harri left her to walk up the hill to Acre Uchaf. He didn't offer to walk with her. It smacked of 'Walking you home' and he had just walked with her. Harri wanted to make sure she'd remember that.

His last words were 'See ya, Suks! Say Hiya to Ni from me!'

Suki did not want to seem scared in front of Harri, so she waited till she couldn't hear his footsteps and then bolted up the hill holding her breath and with both eyes tight shut. The noise of the blood pumping around her head sounded like a thousand footfalls. As she swung the big metal gate open, the noise of the kitchen door made her jump. She was still trembly.

'Suki!' It was Taid on his way out to pick them up. Suki's eyes were as wide as saucers and she was covered with sweat. Taid, and then Nain when she saw her, feared the worst.

When everyone had calmed down Nain and Taid's sympathy subsided and they were just cross.

'She said she'd be back by ten, Nain, honest! It's still only five to. I tried to stop her!'

'She's usually so sensible!' Nain was still with worry. She sat down in Heulwen's chair. 'Well now, what next?'

Then Heulwen woke up and Suki went and sat with her and talked and sang her back to sleep. In the sitting room she could hear Nain and Taid alternately suggesting they phone the police, then that everything would be OK and Nia was very responsible really. They phoned the Parry-Joneses, who reassured them that their daughter was very sensible too, and that Ieuan and Jonathan came from very nice families.

Before real hysteria set in, the phone rang. It was

a very small voice that sounded far away, but was in a village a few miles away. Nain's face relaxed into a smile of relief. 'Oh Nia, love!' Suki and Taid watched in silence, 'He's on his way. Just you wait there!'

Suki was rather briskly packed off to bed, but she couldn't sleep. She heard the car come back and she heard them go in the house. She heard Nain shouting at Nia, and then she heard Nia slam the kitchen door and come into the caravan. She was sobbing, those gaspy sobs you can't stop.

Suki said nothing at first, pretending to be asleep while Nia undressed and got into bed. 'Are you OK?' Nia didn't answer. 'Ni, what happened?'

'Nothing bloody happened! OK?' Nia took a breath in and it turned into a cry.

'Was it one of the boys?'

'No it was bloody not! Just shut up! OK! Shut up!'

Neither could sleep, Suki for wanting to know, Nia too embarrassed to close her eyes.

13

When Suki awoke, she was aware of banging and shouting almost on a level with her ear on the other side of the thin caravan wall. It was the new visitors, a family with a little dog yapping at a growling Monica Rose, and two small children, squealing with delight as they ran around the yard chasing chickens. Suki recognised the mother's ineffectual London suburban drawl, 'Georgia! William! Do stop worrying those poor birds!'

She rolled over and glanced at the little bedside clock. It was nearly eleven. Nia was flat out lying on her back, her eyes black with unwashed make-up, her mouth open, almost snoring. Suki stared at her. It was strange looking at someone asleep, unguarded, like a little child, or a dead body.

Eleven! Oh my God! thought Suki, Lisa's horse!

'Ni! Ni! Get up!'

Nia grunted and grumbled and rolled over, one sleepy hand dragging some more old mascara across her face.

'Nia! Aren't you supposed to get up?' Nia looked at her puzzled. 'That Horse! You know! Your mate with the horse!'

'I don't have a mate with a horse!' Nia growled sleepily, pulling the pillow over her head to block out the light.

'This is exciting!' Suki sat on the edge of Nia's bed dying to know. 'Oh, go on! Tell us! What happened? Please, Ni!'

Nia's voice was not cross, just tired, 'Go away!'

'Oh, Nia, it's not fair! I'll ask Sarah. She'll know! Please, Ni!'

'Just go away!' Suki dressed and left for the house, slamming the flimsy caravan door after her.

Nia lay, fully awake under the pillow, bright white light shining in round the corners. She tried making anagrams of her friends' names, or seeing how many words you could make from the first word that came into your head. But the only words she could think of were 'jeep' and 'sick' and 'public house', and the only names Lisa and Jonathan. She shrivelled with embarrassment as it all began over again.

When it had started, and she was sitting in the back of the jeep and the less than warm air nearly blowing her out of her seat, she'd felt like she was in one of those ads for fizzy drinks or chocolates. She was sitting in the back with Lisa, who was trying not to look put out as her hair blew all over the place. Nia wished Ceri was with her to share it and make it real.

Ieuan seemed very interested in Lisa. Nia found the whole thing entirely embarrassing. She found neither Ieuan or Jonathan good looking, and couldn't believe this was the boy that Lisa had been going on about. Nia thought it must be the car. Both boys wore the same sort of clothes, expensive jeans, the same make that Suki always wore, and long sleeved, clean T-shirts. Ieuan was sort of fair, once a blond baby thought Nia, but nothing special. 'No spots though!' was about as enthusiastic as she had got. Jonathan was smaller, with curly hair. Nia thought it strange that at the dance Lisa had been going on about him too. 'Don't you think Jon's got nice eyes, Ni?' Maybe she was going to ditch Ieuan.

They had gone into town and up the old narrow streets near the centre. Nia knew where they were heading, the big old pub which she had only ever seen from the outside, overflowing with young people, girls in tight dresses and make-up or just jeans and T-shirts, boys that almost looked like men, laughing very loudly so you could hear them from the chip shop over the road.

Nia couldn't believe that no one took any notice when she went in with the others, everyone looked so grown up. Did she really look like everyone else? It was exciting and scary and her stomach was turning over. Nia felt like she was an imposter, a fake—as if the blue dress, in a puff of coloured smoke, would turn back into muddy jodphurs. And Ieuan would turn to Lisa and say 'Look it's that little Nia Roberts!' and Lisa would toss her golden chestnut hair and point and laugh.

But it didn't happen. Nia didn't know what to drink. She knew she didn't like lager, 'cause that was what Rhys drank. Sometimes she'd had wine, but she didn't much like that either. Coke or juice seemed too babyish. Ieuan had to shout above the noise of the pub, 'Come on, Nia, what d'you want?' Nia smiled a very un-Nia like girly smile. 'I'll have the same as you Lisa.'

They found a couple of empty seats and sat down. Lisa lit up a cigarette and offered one to Nia. 'No thanks,' and the boys returned with the drinks.

Jon came and sat next to her, squashing her up against the wall and smiling at her. Nia was embarrassed and sipped her drink. Although it looked like orange juice, it tasted hot and stung her throat a bit. It didn't help having Jonathan trying to talk to her, and Nia shouted 'What?' back at him until he spoke right up against her ear. She still couldn't tell what he was saying but it made a lovely buzzy tickly feeling that went right through her.

It happened when they had left the pub and were going to head back to Ieuan's since his parents were out. Nia had almost forgotten about Taid and Nain and was enjoying herself, laughing at stupid jokes. She felt part of the group, she felt good. Her first mistake was in the car. 'Come on, Lisa, get in the back with me!' She had thumped the seat next to her. But Nia had not noticed that the rules had changed, and Lisa ignored her.

Jonathan had his arm around her shoulder and it felt heavy and squashing like a huge lead bar and suddenly she felt incredibly tired. With each bump and jolt of the car her stomach seemed to move nearer her head. She shut her eyes and hoped the world would go away. However, Jonathan read the closed eyes and the limp body entirely differently. Leaning over, he kissed her. Nia tasted the stale lager and breathed his hot damp breath. She was going to push him away but was overwhelmed by nausea. Jonathan kissed her again.

At school some of the girls talked about French kissing. She had once seen her brother and Beca kissing so hard that you could hear their teeth clanking together. Nia supposed that if you liked the other person enough then it could be enjoyable. But not on two and a half vodka and oranges.

Nia was sick, all over Ieuan's upholstery and all over Jonathan's jeans.

14

Suki sat in the kitchen looking across at the caravan. Nia hadn't moved. She didn't understand Nain either. No one was saying anything. 'She will tell you in her own time,' Nain had said, not looking up from her crossword. 'In the meantime just forget it, there's a good girl.' Suki did not feel like being a 'good girl' —Nia had obviously not been a 'good girl'.

Suki sat at the kitchen table, picking a corner of the Formica up so it curled round like a brandy snap. 'Stop it, Suki!' Nain put down the newspaper. 'Why don't you run and catch up Heulwen? You said you had a nice time at Cornwal Isa.'

'Wow!' But Suki could not think of anything better. At least it was a bike ride with a purpose. And it wasn't raining—'Yet!' said Nain.

As Suki rounded the farmhouse she saw Iola Mary sitting on the wall by the open back door, squinting in the remains of the sunlight. She looked at Suki as if she were the merest speck, 'What are you doing here?'

Suki wanted to say something suitably cutting and aggressive back but only managed, 'I'm seeing Heulwen.'

'Oh.'

Heulwen was off limits. No one, not even Iola or Wendy teased about Heulwen. Silence. Suki hovered by the door of the cowshed. Maybe Iola had heard what had happened.

'Did you enjoy yourself, then? Last night? Seems Nia did.' Iola was fishing too, thought Suki. She shrugged.

'OK. I left early though. You know, wasn't my kind of thing.' Suddenly she felt wicked, 'I came back with Harri.' She tried to sound casual.

'What, in your Taid's car?'

Suki was smiling. 'No, we walked.' She paused, looking Iola straight in the face. 'Together.' Suki couldn't help it. It was lovely to be winding Iola up so successfully. Iola was almost boiling with rage, but said nothing. Suki ran into the shed desperately trying to giggle silently.

When she had composed herself enough to come back out, Iola Mary had gone.

'Heulwen! You should've seen her face!' Suki was desperate to tell someone, but it meant nothing to Heulwen. Nia was probably still too wound up with herself, or in bed. 'Meinir! She'll love it!'

It wasn't until she had almost reached Rhos that it sunk in. Harri was Meinir's brother. He was not going to be at all pleased at being romantically linked with Nia Roberts's little cousin. And having told Iola it would probably be all over the village by now. What did Cecile always say? 'Loose lips sink ships.' And there went Suki's, slipping down into the icy depths and making her stomach turn over and over.

She skidded to a halt. She would cycle back to Cornwal Isa and pretend nothing had happened.

That afternoon there was a storm. Nain swore it had been gathering all week as the weather had got warmer and the air closer. When at last, late in the afternoon, the weather broke and the rain came down, it was like a huge sigh of relief.

All day had been horrible, a thick blanket of cloud, edge to edge across the sky. By lunchtime the clouds were so heavy they seemed almost yellowy grey, sulphurous and nasty.

Heulwen Haf and Suki were out again, and Nia sat outside the caravan playing with Monica Rose. This was very hard work, as Monica Rose was not a gleeful bundle of fluff. Far from it. She would not fetch any ball, wellington boot, or even her rubber ring. To a spectator it looked as if Nia was playing fetch, while Monica Rose, an inert pile of fur, watched. Nia had been told to keep the dog out of the way as Taid had the baler at work today, and Monica Rose was not enamoured of farm machinery. In some ways she was quite like her owner.

'Come on, Mon.' Nia clipped the dog's ancient leather lead onto its collar, and jumped down off the caravan step. 'I'll show you the sea.'

Nia didn't fancy the quicker walk towards the village. The last thing she wanted was to run into Lisa, or her poisonous little sister. So she set out along the track over the top and down to the beach at Porth.

The little town was still quite busy, with the tea room and the handful of souvenir shops mostly full. Full of visitors doggedly wearing their flip-flops and shorts, hoping against hope that the clouds would part and the sun would shine.

But it didn't. The rain started when Nia and Monica Rose were on the beach. Nia was dressed for it, in her old waxed jacket and a pair of Heulwen's calf-length wellies. As Monica trotted along the shore line the few more resilient visitors who had insisted on their picnic tea on the beach, packed up in a flurry of multi-coloured plastic pac-a-macs, Kagoules, Tupperware and thermos flasks, and decamped to their cars in the beach car park.

Nia was not in a hurry. She would walk as far as the last windbreak, then head back home. But the rain was relentless and stung her face and Monica Rose was decidedly unhappy, looking at Nia sideways under her furry eyebrows. 'OK, Mon, I get the message,' Nia was talking out loud to the dog. They headed up the beach to the car park and the high street and the way home.

The lead was still in her jacket pocket. She was going to clip it on when they reached the road, and anyway, Monica Rose was not a frisky light-headed pup, or anything like that. Nia had one hand at her neck, holding the collar of her jacket together where the popper had broken, and the other deep in her pocket. As they walked up the beach the rain seemed, if that was possible, to be getting heavier, the sky darker, iron grey. The cars on the high street had put their lights on.

Monica Rose was a little ahead, not quite running till she reached the car park where she huddled by the back wheel of a car. Nia saw her, looking like a drenched furry blanket. The car was full of ex-picnickers and the windows had steamed up with their hot damp bodies.

Nia saw Monica jump up out of the way when the car engine started. Nia called her, wary of the traffic, 'Come here, girl,' holding out the lead. Monica Rose trotted over towards the familiar voice straight into the path of a reversing car.

Nia ran, the sand slowing her every step like tar, the ridiculous half-mast wellingtons flapping around her shins.

It didn't seem real. She saw the car, a big blue estate, stop and disgorge its passengers, an assortment of different sized children who stood round the dog's damp, twitching body. The driver, a long faced woman, started apologising and the youngest child started crying.

Once, at the stables, a few of the ponies had got loose in the yard, and tried to stampede back to the paddock. The leader of this band of delinquents was a large piebald called Prince. He was a plod, the horse they put the twelve stone novice day trippers from Widnes on. This behaviour was an outburst of repressed exuberance, but it ended in tragedy. Prince had somehow forgotten about the cattle grid and, snorting and bucking, proceeded to gallop gaily over it. Nia had watched as the large animal fell, one foreleg slipping down between the metal rungs. He tried to pull himself out screaming and bellowing in pain. She had never heard a horse screaming before.

She couldn't remember much after that. Just the noise and the sight of the bloody dangling forelimb.

That was all she could think of now, all she saw, even though she was looking at the dog.

'Where's the nearest vet? Does anyone here know? Come on, careful how you lift her, she's still breathing, put her in the back here, that's it.' An English couple with one of those four wheel drive cars seemed to have taken over. Nia couldn't bear to touch the dog in case she was dead.

'There's a vet in Nefyn.' Nia's voice was flat.

'Come on, then, get in quickly!' The man seemed to be enjoying the drama. The woman put her arm protectively around Nia and ushered her into the back seat.

'Don't worry, love I'm sure she'll be all right.'

She smiled weakly at Nia, but Nia didn't answer. She just stared silently out to the wet car window, already imagining how she was going to tell Heulwen.

15

On Sunday it was still raining. The water gathered in the ditches at the side of the road and swooshed down to the village on one side of the hill, and to the sea on the other. Nain, Taid and Heulwen had gone to chapel. Suki had gone too, which was unusual, but then she and Heulwen Haf had been thick as thieves all week, and besides, Suki said she'd fancied the singing.

Nia was in no mood for company. She could not bear the way Heulwen had looked at her at breakfast, eyes widening, then blubbing and gasping inconsolably, holding Monica Rose's old chewed lead against her chest like some talisman. Nia had said sorry a hundred times. Nain had told her it wasn't her fault.

But Heulwen had just sobbed louder, rocking in her chair, refusing to eat. Nia had snapped, shouting, 'I've told you a hundred times, SHE IS NOT DEAD, can't you understand? IT WASN'T MY FAULT AND SHE IS NOT DEAD!' But of course Heulwen did not really understand and Nia shouting at her just made it worse. And now Nain, Taid and Suki were angry with her for not 'making allowances', and Nia felt like the worst person in the world.

She sat on her bed hugging her knees, 'The vet said she would be all right,' she muttered out loud to herself. 'No, will be all right.' She was trying to reassure herself.

She looked out over the yard from the caravan. She could see the visitors resplendent in fluorescent Kagoules flapping between the caravan and their car, armed with binoculars, camera and packed lunch. That at least made her smile. She flopped onto her bed and searched under it for a book from her holdall.

But she couldn't concentrate. Her throat was all choky from trying not to cry, and her thoughts strayed from the book to Monica Rose and if she managed to forget the dog then it was Lisa Parry-Jones.

She would go into the house and phone the vet, just to make sure.

Inside the house she put the kettle on and switched on the telly, anything to blot out the thoughts in her head. The vet's had an answering machine but she couldn't leave a message. She made herself a cup of tea and sat curled up in Heulwen's chair. On the telly a vicar was preaching about the family of God, then the congregation started singing and Nia turned the telly off.

The television sat on a fat squat chest of drawers, overflowing with bits of paper. The top one was full of household bills and stuff, tax forms, pension books and the like. In the bottom two were photos. Nia sat down in front of it and pulled the drawer right out onto the floor. There were loads of pictures all jumbled up: Nain and Taid getting married, in the lane with all the family; Dilys and Heulwen, dressed identically, with her mother, Ceinwen, in some sort of archaic pushchair. Even her old school photos. Her mother's Sunday School exam certificates. She'd seen them all before.

Nia was about to put the drawer back in when she noticed what looked like a scrap of paper at the back of the cupboard. She pulled it out. It read, 'To my dear Sara, yours, Friedrich Groeger, September 1944'. She turned it over, and there smiling at her was a tanned young man leaning against a tree. He didn't look in the least bit Welsh. Friedrich not Frederick. Wasn't it German? He wore one of those army type caps without a peak. She turned it over and read the writing again, then she looked at the photo again.

Nia smiled. She couldn't imagine Nain, her Nain, her old Nain, having a boyfriend! But the date was 1944. She rifled through the other photos. Here was the wedding, here was a newspaper clipping, here were the good luck telegrams. Here was a small, old, white card with a crinkly silver edge and silver embossed letters; 'You are invited to the wedding of Owen John Gruffudd and Sara Price,' then the chapel and the time, then the date '20th of May, 1939.'

Nia held the photos together and looked at them both. Taid didn't stand a chance, she thought. She put them all back in the drawer and turned the telly on again: it was a sign language programme. Nia went back to the kitchen and started buttering toast, idly watching the telly through the serving hatch. It was a school for deaf teenagers in East Berlin. Germany. Friedrich, what was it? Yes, Groeger. She smiled. Then the tiniest stupid little thought shot through her mind. She stopped smiling. Nia put down her knife and went back and opened the drawer.

She pulled out the photographs, one of Aunty Dilys, Heulwen, and her Mum, Ceinwen, all in their Sunday Best. Heulwen hadn't changed a bit! But she and Dilys were slighter and darker and Ceinwen's fairer hair seemed almost white in the black and white picture. She looked at the date on the back— 'Sept 1950.' Her mother would have been six, her Aunts ten. 'Don't be stupid!' she said it out loud, mockingly. But all the same she rummaged about and found the soldier, still propping up his tree. It was hard to really see his face in the small wrinkled photo. It was a sunny day and the shadows were strong, but it could be, maybe . . . She didn't want to think of it, and stuffed the photos quickly back in the drawer. She hoped her ridiculous idea had gone too.

But it seemed to explain so much! Nia's mind raced as she began to piece it all together in her head. 'Mum always got the raw deal, she never got the chance to go to University! Yes! It's always how great Dilys's job is, or how Heulwen's getting on! Never Mum!' Nia paced the sitting room trying to keep up with her thoughts. 'Always Dilys or Heulwen! Never Mum! And she's taller than them! Yes!' It all seemed so obvious.

Nia went to look in the mirror in Nain's bedroom and studied her face. There, smiling on the dresser, were pictures of her aunts, and one of Taid taken last summer. Even she and Rhys in school. She checked every proportion, every arch of eyebrow and angle of jaw. She felt the picture she had of herself slipping quickly and silently away. She wanted to cry but nothing happened. Nothing at all.

She stared at the reflection in the mirror and it felt as if she was looking at someone else.

The phone rang. Nia froze, then quickly ran through into the sitting room shoving all the 'evidence' back into the drawer before she picked the phone up. 'Hello?' it came out trembly and weak. Did they know what she had been doing? Thinking?

'Hello? Is that Acre Uchaf, Rhos? The Gruffudds?' The voice on the other end was super cheerful, every pause ended on an up note, like an over-attentive waitress in a hamburger bar.

'Yes . . . well, they're not in . . .' Nothing. '. . . can I take a message?'

'Oh Yes! If you would. It's about the dog, Monica Rose, isn't it?'

Nia's skin paled from grey to palest green, and to make things worse she could hear Taid and Nain and Heulwen and Suki come squeaking through the metal farm gate.

Suki and Heulwen and Nain were walking, arms linked, Heulwen in the middle looking as vulnerable and lost as a small child. Her eyes were ringed red with weeping through the hymns at chapel. Suki hadn't been able to follow what the minister had said but his almost theatrical intonation, and the atmosphere, had been enough for her to get lost and almost weepy when the singing started up.

As they walked towards the house they could see Nia through Nain's big 'picture window' on the phone. In a second Nia had put the phone down and was at the doorway almost jumping up and down.

'She's all right! She is all right!' Nia ran to Heulwen Haf and hugged her 'It's all right! She'll be home on Wednesday! Wednesday, Heul! Three days!'

16

It was the happy ending that everyone had wanted. After the extra special celebratory Sunday lunch had worn off, Nia sat in front of the telly and felt as if she was in a plastic bubble. She had never felt so apart from her own family before. They didn't even feel much like her family. They didn't know anything. She was seething with crossness and no one seemed to notice.

Nain, Taid and Heulwen were going out, driving to Caernarfon to see some friends. It was still raining. Nia switched the telly on. Suki was sitting at the dining table with a drawing pad on her lap. Arranged in front of her was her still life, a sheep's skull she had found at Cornwal Isa.

'If you're putting that thing on my table, get some newspaper under it! Now!' Nain had said, as Suki had added some rusty bracken in a clump, and a big lump of rock.

Nia looked over at Suki's 'foreign' profile, her froth of hair, big curving forehead, squashy button nose and too-thick-to-be-white lips. Nia had always been jealous of Suki's looks: she was glamorous, exotic. But maybe that wasn't such a plus. Nia thought she felt something of the otherness that Suki felt. That separateness that she must feel, even with Nain and Taid. A bit of her that had nothing to do with greyness and coldness and rain.

'Oi! What are you staring at?'

Nia jumped. 'Nothing! Really!'

Suki went back to her drawing. Nia flicked the telly off, listening to the scraping of Suki's pencil across paper. Maybe she could talk to her.

'Listen, Suks.'

'Hmm?'

Before she could continue, Nia noticed a tall bedraggled figure open the big gate and cross the yard. For a second her stomach did somersaults as she imagined it was Jonathan, then instantly relaxed as she realised who it was.

'Thank God! It's only Harri!'

Suki froze. 'What?' She saw him too. She couldn't tell if he just looked grim from being wet or what. 'Oh no! I'm not here! Tell him! Really, Nia! Really!'

Nia was interested. 'Don't be stupid! He can see you through the window! Anyway, how do you know he's come to see you?' She was already going to the kitchen door to open it. 'Harri!'

Harri shook himself over the doormat, dripping onto the lino and easing his trainers off without bending down.

Suki hovered in the sitting room. It was ridiculous trying to pretend she wasn't there. She sat down again and doodled anxiously on the edge of her sketchbook. It felt like waiting to see the headmistress.

Nia was pleased to see him—it was a welcome distraction. 'Do you want some tea? Coffee?'

'No, thanks.'

Harri was trying to keep the angry feeling that he'd left home with. On the walk over he had started to see the funny side, and there was almost nothing left to be cross about. But he wanted to tell Suki off, and he wanted to see Nia.

Suki was sitting, knees pulled up, on the edge of her chair. She didn't look up, she just stared intently at the flaky sheep skull, pencil in hand hovering just above the surface of the paper. As if she were about to do something important.

'Aren't you going to say hello?' Nia smiled. 'Harri's here!'

Suki still didn't look up. 'You sound like my mother!' She paused. 'Hello, Harri.'

Then there was silence. Nia was sitting on the arm of the sofa, smirking. Harri smouldered in the armchair, perfecting his 'tough-but-wounded' look then sniffed, then silence again. 'Well!' said Nia at last, unable to contain herself, 'Will one of you tell me what's going on, or shall I go in the kitchen and listen behind the door? Oh come on, I'm dying to know.'

Suki still said nothing. Harri cleared his throat.

'Your cousin over there, Nia, has been putting it about that me and her'—he did his best contemptuous head toss in Suki's direction—'have been meeting every day since that bloody dance,' he paused a little for breath, 'to snog in that old barn over by Cornwal Isa!'

Suki exploded with indignation, glad that she could deny it all with a clear conscience. 'Ooh! That is a bloody buggering lie! I would no sooner snog with you than with that bloody cow of Heulwen's.'

Nia was giggling so much she fell off the sofa.

'Well I don't think it's that funny!' Suki wanted to make out she was as offended as Harri.

Harri looked at Nia creased up on the floor, and at Suki opening and shutting her mouth like an outraged guppy. He started laughing too. Nia climbed back onto the sofa. 'I bet Iola's cross!'

'Iola had the nerve to tell me I had led her on!'

'Had you?' Nia asked.

'Me and Io!' Harri laughed even more, 'I rang her up a couple of times to see if she could baby sit when I had football practice! I've wished I hadn't ever since!'

'Poor Iola!' Nia was a bit sorry for her.

'Poor Iola nothing! I can't wait till school goes back and they've got other things to think about!'

Suki had begun to giggle too, mostly with relief. She would just slide away and no one would notice.

'Hey! Suki!' Harri turned round to face her, 'Don't do it again.'

Suki went bright red. 'Look! I am thirteen, not bloody nine! You believe what you bloody want!'

Suki ran through the kitchen and slammed the door, shaking the cups in the cupboard.

'Oh, don't worry!' Nia didn't move.

'I'm not,' Harri answered, honestly.

'It's ninety per cent show, she's, um, what does Aunty Dilys call it? A real Drama Queen!'

'I've noticed!' Harri got up. 'Anyway, I'd better go.'

'Yeah and I should go and sort her out.' Nia looked out, across to the caravan.

'You know, I heard what happened with you the other night.'

Nia put both hands up to her face. 'Arrghh! So it's all over the place now, is it?'

'Well,' Harri continued, 'you should be grateful to me and Suki for knocking "Nia Roberts is sick on son of magistrate" off the top talking point spot!'

'Thanks!' Nia did not sound convinced.

Harri had found his jacket, which was still wringing wet, so Nia offered him Taid's pacamac.

'Listen,' Harri sounded serious.

'What?' Nia wasn't listening, she was trying to arrange the wet jacket over the radiator.

Harri coughed, 'Are you busy on Friday night?'

'What?'

Harri was beginning to blush. Nia looked at him slightly puzzled.

'I said, are you busy on Friday night?'

Nia looked at him as if he was soft in the head.

'Look,' said Harri, 'you're not making me say it again!'

'Are you asking me out?'

'Only to the cinema at Pwllheli!'

'Really? Not afraid I'll vomit all over you?'

'I'm used to it. Iolo does it all the time!'

'I don't believe you!'

'No! It's true, if he eats too many jelly babies!'

'Not that, you idiot!"

'Why not?'

'Oh, Harri! I can't go, can I? They're definitely not going to let me go after last week!'

'S'pose not!' Harri started pulling on his squelchy trainers. 'I'm busy with Iolo until the weekend. It's not much of a date with a pushchair!'

'We're going home next Saturday,'

'Oh well, that's that.' Harri was fiddling with the door handle.

Nia smiled at him. 'Thanks for asking. Really!'

Harri squelched out, and Nia watched, smiling at him as he set off down the hill.

Nia went into the kitchen and made herself some tea. She was grinning broadly. That was the first time anyone had asked her out. Jonathan was different, she was pretending that had never happened, and so was Geraint at school—he had asked nearly everyone in her year. Oh, and Tom down the road didn't count either because everyone knew they had been friends for ages, and it was always as a gang with lots of others, and only in the winter when most of the ponies were turned out on the mountain.

She finished making the tea, and took a can of fizzy something out to the caravan to cheer up Suki.

'You'll never guess!'

'Amazing!' Suki answered sarcastically. 'You're actually going to tell your baby cousin something! Are you sure I can handle it?'

'Oh don't be like that! Here.' And she threw Suki the can.

'Oh Nia! It'll go everywhere now!'

Nia cradled her mug of tea, 'I'm really glad he asked me!'

Suki sniffed, 'Boy wonder!'

'Oh God, though . . .' Nia continued, not really taking any notice of Suki. 'I don't think I could face actually going out with him! This way, it's like,' she paused, picking at the hole in her sock, 'like, being able to pick all the sticky-up bits of icing off a Christmas cake without having to eat that awful fruit cake stuff underneath!' Nia sighed, happily. 'But, honestly, Suki! Making that stuff up!' Nia leant forward. 'Did you fancy him? For someone so supposedly clever as you, you really can be grade one stupid!' Nia smiled and sipped her tea.

'Don't talk to me like that!' Suki was furious.

'Like what!'

'You know, that smug, "older cousin" bit! You're not my mother!'

Nia was cross too now. 'Well at least I don't have to make things up just to get attention!'

'I didn't say those things!'

But Nia wasn't listening. She had gone back in the house and Suki was back on her own.

17

The next morning the rain had stopped and the sun sparkled in the pools of upside down sky in the yard. Nia hadn't slept at all well. She had wriggled and turned, winding herself up in the sheet so that it took an awful lot of effort just to pull her body free of the bed and get up.

Suki snored deeply, the sound sleep of the unworried, thought Nia, and pulled on her boots. Apart from feeling confused and alienated, she was missing Louie, the pony. There was no point in saying it out loud to anyone except Ceri. They would think she was daft.

Nia didn't fancy seeing Lisa and she was sure the feeling would be mutual. But with any luck, no one would be about yet at Ty'n Llidiart.

She didn't feel like cycling so she walked, cross country, by the footpath that ran south east from the bottom field. It was deceptively muddy.

As Nia approached the field she could see Louie raise his head from the grass and sniff the air, curling back his top lip so you could see all his teeth. Nia called out to him, as softly as possible, and made little clicking noises to coax him over. It didn't need much. In a few seconds he was cantering over towards her, and in a few seconds more crunching happily on Polos.

'So it's cupboard love, is it?' and she tickled him behind his ears. Louie bent his neck over the wire fence and rested his half ton head in her arms. One thing about horses, Nia thought to herself, they always listen, not like bloody sulky Suki.

Louie whickered at her and Nia wondered if maybe, just maybe, Lisa would have her back. Louie did look a bit scruffy, his once white socks now brown and his mane and tail all tangled. It might be worth a try.

Maybe if she went quietly round the back and

made up the haynets like she used to . . . And if she got Louie in and cleaned him up. 'Yes, why not, eh? You'd like that, wouldn't you, sausage?'

So Nia stole around to the back of the house and started shoving handfuls of damp hay into Louie's co-ordinating bright blue haynet.

She had just taken the grooming kit out and was about to fetch the pony in when she heard muffled shouts, then loud banging. It was Lisa, thumping on her bedroom window. Nia couldn't really make out the expression on her face because the sun was bouncing off the glass, part reflecting sky and grass. Nia smiled hopefully and waved Louie's headcollar up at the high window. She didn't want to shout in case she woke Lisa's parents.

Then there was nothing. The figure had gone and Nia stopped squinting up at the window, shrugged, and started over to the paddock. As she led the pony back to the yard the kitchen door swung open, and Lisa strode out, still in a T-shirt and dressing gown, her orange hair flopping shinily over her shoulders.

Nia waved at her rather lamely. 'Hi!' she said out loud, but inside she was trying desperately to work out what Lisa would most like to hear, and her stomach was making evil gurgling noises, reminding her that she hadn't had any breakfast.

'What the hell do you think you're doing? I thought someone was trying to steal him!' She pulled the lead rope sharply out of Nia's hands, causing Louie's head to jerk forward sharply.

'Careful!' Nia hadn't meant to say it at all, let

alone as sharply as it had come out. Lisa looked fiercely at her.

'He's my pony!' and led him back to the field and turned him out again, picking over the mud in a pair of furryslippers.

'I thought I'd give you a hand.' Ni sounded unconvinced. Lisa glared.

'What I want to know,' barked Lisa as she rounded up her hair into a ponytail, 'is where've you been the last couple of days! I thought you cared about him! You should have phoned! Look at those feet now!' She pointed over to the paddock. 'He'll probably get mud fever or something!'

Nia sighed, but it was going to be OK. All she would have to do was grovel a bit. Lisa just wanted to tell her off, make sure she knew her place, then Nia could get back to work.

'To tell the truth,' Nia didn't look up, 'it was after that business with Jonathan, you know! I thought—,'

'Yes!' Lisa was losing patience.

'I thought, well I couldn't really face seeing you.' Nia smiled stupidly. 'It was so embarrassing!'

'You were embarrassed! Hah! What about me?' Lisa tossed her pony-tail.

'I'm sorry!' Nia kicked about the loose gravel with her toe.

Lisa went on, 'I thought you were my friend!'

Nia looked up. That sounded so stupid but she kept her mouth shut.

'I should have known someone like you is only interested in horses!' Lisa pulled the tie belt of her dressing gown tighter and turned to go back into the house. 'Come back when you've grown up!'

That was it, Nia thought, breathing in to feel stronger. 'You know what?'

'What?' Lisa wasn't even looking at her

'You don't deserve that pony.'

Lisa's jaw dropped a metre.

'You are a stuck up cow and I pity poor Louie having to cart you around while you jab him in the mouth and hit him.' Lisa was speechless. 'Also,' Nia breathed in again, 'you are a spoilt brat and I will be glad if I never see you again!' One more breath and Nia walked away.

Nia's eyes were streaming so much she could hardly see out of them. She walked down the drive sniffing, but as quietly as she could, then as soon as she was out of earshot, and out of sight of either the house or the road, she let go.

18

Puffy-eyed, Nia looked around. She was in the old camp in the field next door to Ty'n Llidiart, huddled up against one of the old concrete graffiti-covered pillars, sitting on the concrete floor of one of the huts. She picked a bit of moss. She didn't want to go back, not now, not ever. She would never be rich, like Lisa, and anyway, those other people, they were only half her family. She imagined Friedrich Groeger, her real *taid*, sitting in an office somewhere in Germany, with a big blonde wife with plaits up on her head. They had a BMW and a big house. With horses, of course. The Germans were good at horses.

Why had no one ever told her? Did her mother know?

The sun had made the concrete warm already and, if she lay almost flat, she could see Louie in the other field through the gap. She was wondering if her *taid* had slept here, and up in the sky the swallows were diving and chasing. Her stomach rumbled. She stretched out a bit more on the warm stone.

After lunch Nain was getting worried. 'Nia was up before you, then, love?' She didn't actually tell Suki she was worried, but Suki could tell, from the way Nain put her hand on Suki's shoulder a little longer than usual, and took less notice of Heulwen than she should.

'Look, Nain,' Suki stood up and tried to sound as dynamic as possible, 'she's probably made it up with Lisa Whatsit-Jones and is happily scooping up as much horse pooh as she can handle, at this very moment.'

Nain didn't seem convinced. But Suki thought she'd go and have a look anyway.

Suki had no intention of actually going to the house, just a look in the field, and maybe at the back. Anyway, it was nice to be out after all that rain. The caravan walls had seemed to be growing closer over the weekend.

Suki passed the house once without realising she'd missed it. She got as far as the new village sign and had had to double back. You couldn't really miss the place either, screened from the road by a massive curtain of some kind of evergreen trees—the paddock, too, with its screaming orange shelter.

And there, just visible, was Lisa, looking cross as she tried to brush off what looked like acres of mud attached to the poor pony's hooves and ankles. But no Nia. Suki kept out of sight. She didn't want to make small, or any other sort of talk.

Suki had given up and was heading back up the road when something caught her eye in amongst the concrete stumps of the neighbouring field. It was so ridiculous that she kept cycling past it. It was only when she got back to the junction by the shop that she realised she should go back and have a proper look. Suki thought of asking Sarah to come with her, but she knew Sarah would think she was being silly. Suki had thought she saw a hand.

Suki rode back. It was still there. She left her bike at the side of the road and crossed the fence where the wire had been pulled right down. She stumbled more than once on lumps of concrete and brick hidden in the long grass. As she got nearer she could see it wasn't a man's hand, or even a particularly large one.

Was it part of a dismembered corpse lying scattered around? Had she already tripped over the head, or the torso? She froze in the middle of the field, hardly daring to tread one more step. She was as far from the bike as she was from the hand. Heart thumping, she realised it was sort of twitching. It looked strangely familiar, especially now she could see a frayed, browny olive cuff, and as she unfroze and came nearer she felt a wash of relief that it was only Nia.

For a moment that, and the movement, had steadied Suki's nerve. But when she saw Nia's puffy looking eyes, and the tiny trail of dribble from her open mouth, she was worried again. Suki could see Nia's chest rising and falling, so she wasn't dead, but was it concussion? Or maybe she'd hit her head.

'Nia!' Suki was shaking her shoulder. 'Nia! Wake up! Please, Nia!'

By the time Nia had shown signs of waking up, Suki was seriously frightened. Tears squeezing out of the corners of her eyes.

Nia sat up. Suki hugged her, hastily wiping most of the tears on Nia's back, so she wouldn't know she had been crying. Nia rubbed her eyes too.

'What are you doing here?'

'Looking for you, actually!'

'Oh no!' Nia felt her arm numb, where it had been squashed by her body. 'I wasn't asleep, was I?' Nia sat up, bending her neck around to get rid of the ache.

'I had a row with Lisa.' Nia squinted up at Suki.

'I thought you already had!' Suki sat down on the concrete floor next to her. It looked as though they were adrift on a raft in a sea of grass.

'Last time I just showed her up; this time, we had the row.'

'Oh!' Suki looked at Nia, crumpled, fuzzy with sleep and red-eyed. 'I'm sorry.'

'It was my own fault.' Nia stretched some more. 'I suppose I knew what she was like.'

Suki looked at her sideways. 'Oh yeah?'

'Horses don't choose their owners. Anyway, it was worth it, being able to ride out on my own.'

'Oh.' Suki was sitting dangling her feet into the grass, idly pulling off the seed heads.

'You've got no idea!' Nia looked into her cousin's face. 'Being able to go off, whenever you like, out on your own, up the mountain,' Nia sighed, 'anywhere!'

To Suki, the thought of being stuck halfway up a mountain sitting on top of some unpredictable, uncontrollable animal did not feel the way Nia looked.

Nia sat up, smiling. 'You've really got no idea at all, have you?'

Suki said 'Sorry' again, but this time it sounded more like she meant it.

They sat in silence for a few minutes, listening to the wind in the grass, and the occasional passing crow. Suki spoke first.

'Sarah told me.'

'What?' Nia sounded guilty. 'You know! That stuff with Jonathan!'

Nia lay back and rolled over, groaning.

Suki giggled. 'I was amazed you had to get drunk before you puked on him!' Suki laughed loudly at her own joke and soon both girls were lying back on the concrete giggling loudly.

'I wish you'd told me though!'

Nia looked at her. 'Sorry!'

Suki continued, 'I've felt really shut out these last few days!'

'Well, you've been off with Heulwen all the time!' Nia sounded hurt.

'Come off it, Ni!' replied Suki. 'You could've come!'

Nia didn't look up.

'Suki?'

'Hmm?'

Both girls were lying still, soaking up the warm sun.

'You know what you said, at my house, about not wanting to come this year?'

'So?'

'You said it like you meant it.'

'Just growing up, I suppose.'

'Come off it!'

'Well do you really want to know?' Suki sat up.

'Yes, actually!'

'I am fed up with being the odd one out. I know what they're saying, those people in the shops in town! They always think I don't understand! I am fed up with explaining who my parents are, and I am fed up with always seeing the funny side!'

Suki's voice had gone shaky and her eyes were watering. She got up and jumped off the concrete and waded through the waving grass towards her bike.

'Suki!' Nia got up after her.

'And worst of all,' Suki shouted back as loud as she could, 'I am fed up with wanting to belong!'

Nia ran and caught her up. Suki was wheeling her bike along with one hand and wiping her nose with the other.

'I'm sorry, Ni!'

'Don't be.'

'So long as you don't say "I know what it's like!".'

They wheeled the bike back up the hill. Suki breathed deeply. She felt better for saying it out loud. She smiled and Nia smiled back at her.

Nia's head seemed clear too, for the first time since last week. All she had to do was ask Nain about the photo. It wouldn't be easy, but at least then she would know. Either way it had to be better. She smiled at her own stupidity.

They had reached the crest of the hill and in front of them the tarmac'd road exploded with tussocks of grass. The wind blew in from the sea onto their faces.

'It's lovely!' Nia spiralled round taking in the view, from the mountains in the east to the sea on every other side.

Suki grinned, 'Even if I don't belong,' she said softly, so softly that her words had gone away with the wind before Nia had heard them, 'this belongs to me!'

Other Pont titles which will appeal to teenage readers:

Time Loft Clare Cooper
Science fiction, set in the Taff valley in the twenty second century. Two girls kidnap Jason Williams who, though no angel in his own time, finds the courage and will to deal with the robotic Designators without becoming evil himself.
£4.25
ISBN 1 85902 144 1

The Hare and Other Stories Catherine Fisher
Four sinister and magical stories, also available on audio-cassette.
£3.25
ISBN 1 85902 181 6

The Magic Apostrophe Jenny Sullivan
Tanith Williams considers herself to be an ordinary Welsh schoolgirl but on her thirteenth birthday is told that she is a witch. It is not all fun . . .
£4.95
ISBN 1 85902 116 6

The Island of Summer Jenny Sullivan
(sequel to *The Magic Apostrophe*). Tanith is now fifteen and once again caught up in the struggle between Good and Evil. Her arch-opponent, Astarte Perkins, with her one blue and one brown eye, is easy to recognise and difficult to avoid!
£4.95
ISBN 1 85902 351 7

Something's Burning Mary Oldham
Barbara Dawes, an incomer to Wales, yearns to be Welsh, to be thin, to have a boyfriend. Heledd Aeronwy Jones, the silent and mysterious girl from north Wales, yearns for less ordinary things and is obviously desperately unhappy.
£4.95
ISBN 1 85902 119 0

The Blue Man and Other Stories From Wales
ed. Christine Evans
15 very different stories about growing up in Wales. Stories include 'Tadpoles' by Catherine Johnson and the title-story, 'The Blue Man', by poet Gillian Clarke.
£4.50
ISBN 1 85902 228 6

POETRY
Are You Talking to Me? Ed. Mairwen Jones & John Spink
Poems on themes that are important to young people from
> Mike Jenkins
> Penny Windsor
> Christine Evans
> Owen Sheers
> John Tripp

£3.95
ISBN 1 85902 178 6